Hacking the PM Interview

Your Shortcut Guide to Mastering Product Manager Interviews

Taylor Warfield

ISBN-13: 978-1-7333381-2-7

Table of Contents

1. Introduction

What is the goal of this book?

Product manager interviews are hard. There is an incredibly wide range of questions that you could get asked, such as product design questions, strategy questions, execution questions, behavioral questions, and technical questions to name a few.

On top of that, competition is fierce. There are many more people interested in product management than there are positions available. Companies have the luxury of being extremely selective and choosy in who they want to hire.

The goal of this book is to prepare you for product manager interviews, give you a competitive advantage among your peers, and maximize the likelihood that you'll land a PM job offer.

To do this, we emphasize three principles that most other PM interview books and resources fall short on.

The first principle is comprehensiveness. We've done our research to ensure that almost any question you could get asked in your PM interviews is covered in this book.

After reading this book, there should be no surprises during any of your upcoming PM interviews.

The second principle is teaching only the most robust and effective strategies. Using generic strategies or following generic interview tips will not work for PM interviews.

We will teach you specific, actionable strategies and techniques that will help you distinguish yourself from other candidates.

The third principle is teaching in the most efficient way possible to save you hundreds of hours of prep time. No one wants to be spending their weekends and holidays preparing for PM interviews.

We will avoid including long anecdotal stories, fluff, and repeating ourselves in any of our content.

With these three principles, we hope that this book is the very best PM interview prep book on the market.

How is this book organized?

We have organized this book by the eleven different categories of PM interview questions:

- Define Yourself Questions
- Motivational Questions
- Behavioral Questions
- Product Questions
- Marketing Questions

- Estimation Questions
- Strategy Questions
- Metrics Questions
- Execution Questions
- Technical Questions
- Take-Home Assignments

For each category of question, we'll define the question, understand what interviewers are looking for, learn the most effective strategies, and practice with real interview questions from a wide range of companies.

If you are ready to start preparing for PM interviews, feel free to move onto the next chapter to start learning right away.

For the remainder of this chapter, we'll provide a concise introduction to product management. This may be helpful for those who are new or unfamiliar with PM.

What is product management?

Product management (PM) is the process of planning, creating, and selling a product. It involves figuring out what the product should do, how it should look, and how to get people interested in using it.

Product managers work with many different teams, such as engineering, design, marketing, sales, finance, and legal, to ensure everything goes smoothly from the idea stage to launch.

After launch, product managers will track how the product is doing and make further improvements if needed.

PM roles encompass a wide range of responsibilities, including:

- Conducting market research to understand customer needs, market trends, and competition, which will guide product development and help make informed decisions
- Defining the product's vision, strategy, and roadmap by setting goals, prioritizing features, and aligning the product with the company's overall business objectives
- Defining product features and requirements to specify what the product should do and how it should behave
- Overseeing development and engineering to ensure that the product is developed according to specifications and timelines
- Working closely with UX/UI designers to ensure that the product is user-friendly, visually appealing, and aligned with the company's brand
- Planning and executing the product launch, including creating marketing strategies, promotional materials, and coordinating with sales teams
- Tracking product performance using metrics and analytics to evaluate the product's success and areas for improvement
- Collecting feedback from customers, sales teams, and other stakeholders to identify areas for improvement
- Acting as a bridge between various departments, such as engineering, marketing, sales, and customer support to ensure everyone is aligned on goals and priorities
- Planning product end-of-life, including decisions regarding discontinuation, migration, or replacement

Not all PM roles are exactly the same. There is quite a wide range of what PM roles look like.

For example, some PM roles are responsible for an entire product while others are responsible for only one feature of a particular product.

Additionally, different PM roles may focus on different stages of the product. Some PM roles focus on working on the early stages of a product, such as conducting market research and defining the product's vision, strategy, and roadmap. Other PM roles focus on planning product end-of-life.

Lastly, different PM roles may have different functional focuses. Some PM roles might be more focused on product marketing, such as creating marketing strategies and coordinating with sales teams. Other PM roles may be more focused on design or product development and engineering.

Why work in product management?

There are many reasons why so many people are interested in product management.

- **Cross-functional collaboration**: PMs get to work with various teams, including engineering, design, marketing and sales, which makes the work more dynamic and interesting

- **Problem solving**: PMs get to solve complex problems that are intellectually stimulating and rewarding

- **Innovation and creativity**: PMs have the opportunity to create something new and innovative, shaping the direction of a product from its features to its user experience

- **Customer-centric focus**: PMs are focused on understanding and meeting customer needs, leading to products that genuinely improve people's lives

- **Entrepreneurial spirit**: PMs act as mini-CEOs of their products, giving them ownership for the success of the product, which can be very entrepreneurial in nature
- **Impact**: Depending on the scale and reach of their products, PMs may have the opportunity to influence markets and industries on a global scale
- **Professional development**: The challenges, responsibilities, and experiences of product management can lead to tremendous personal growth and development
- **Compensation**: PMs are generally very well compensated at companies and are one of the highest paying roles
- **Highly transferable skills**: The skills gained in product management, such as strategic thinking, problem solving, communication, and leadership can be applied to various industries and roles
- **Exit Opportunities**: Experience in product management can lead to a wide range of career paths, including executive leadership roles, entrepreneurship, or consulting

What does the PM interview process look like?

The PM interview process can vary significantly depending on both the company and tenure of the role you are applying for. There is no single interview process that all companies follow.

However, the most common PM interview process will look something like the following:

1. **Resume submission**: You will submit your resume to the job posting on the company's website. A referral from someone that works at the company can greatly improve the likelihood that your application gets considered. Most companies use a combination of software algorithms and

manual resume reviews to determine if your resume is a good match.

2. **Phone screening**: A recruiter, someone in HR, or the hiring manager will schedule an initial phone call with you. They may ask a few questions about your background, discuss your interests in product management, or discuss your interests in the company.

3. **First round interviews**: You will be given 1-2 interviews conducted through phone or video conference. If you are recruiting from school, your first round interviews may take place on campus. These interviews will have a mix of questions, including product, behavioral, strategy, and technical questions.

4. **Final round interviews**: You will be given anywhere from 3 to 6 in-person interviews. These interviews will also have a mix of different types of questions.

5. **Offer decision**: You should expect to receive your offer within a few days or a few weeks following your final round interview.

Regardless of what the interview process looks like, you can prepare for any PM interview by preparing for all of the different types of questions you could get asked.

Bonus Tip: If possible, try to schedule all of your final round interviews within the same few days. If you receive multiple offers, you'll be able to leverage them against each other to get a higher total compensation.

2. Conducting Company Research

Why do you need to do company research?

Before going into your interviews, you should research the company that you are interviewing for. There are two main reasons for this.

One, knowing the company well demonstrates your interest in the company or role. If you show up to an interview without any understanding of what the company does, interviewers will think that you are not interested or serious about the role.

Two, thoroughly researching the company allows you to speak intelligently when asked interview questions. For product and strategy questions, having background knowledge of the company will significantly improve your answer.

By thoroughly researching the company, you can differentiate yourself from the other candidates that only have a basic or no knowledge of what the company does.

You do not need to research every fact about the company. You can easily spend hundreds of hours reading articles, press releases, and analyst reports. Instead, you should be smart in your research and focus on learning only the most important things.

Where do I do company research?

There are four major sources of information you should look into when conducting company research:

1. Company annual report
2. Online articles
3. Current and former employees
4. Analyst reports

Company annual report

All public companies are required to file an annual report on their financial performance called the 10-K. You can find this document under "Investor Relations" on company websites or the SEC government website.

The 10-K is a comprehensive document and a great starting point to learn about the company. Useful information you'll find in a 10-K include:

- Products and services
- Financial performance
- Major competitors
- Recent significant events
- Risks to the business

If the company is private and does not have a 10-K, they may still publish some kind of annual report for their investors that you can look at.

Online articles

The second source of information are online articles, which provide news and perspectives on companies from an outsider or third-party perspective.

In contrast, the 10-K is a report that comes from the company itself. Therefore, the information in online articles will be much more subjective.

You can find online articles by searching for the company name on search engines.

From online articles, you'll find useful information on companies such as:

- Recent significant events
- Perspectives on how these events impact customers, competitors, and the company's future
- Viewpoints on how well the company is performing
- Opinions on what the company should be doing differently

Reading online articles will help you develop a perspective or viewpoint on the company beyond the objective information that the 10-K provides.

Current and former employees

Before interviewing, you should try to speak to at least one person that is a current or former employee of the company that you are interviewing for.

Ideally, try to talk to someone that currently or previously worked in the exact role you are interviewing for.

Speaking to current or former employees will give you valuable information on:

- The culture of the company
- Skills or attributes the company values
- The fit of the role within the broader organization
- The responsibilities and tasks of the role
- Working styles of people on the team

You will likely not find much information on these topics online, so use your network to find someone to talk to.

Analyst reports

Analyst reports are written by financial analysts to provide investment guidance to investors.

Analyst reports are found through online platforms such as Thomson Reuters, Morningstar, Standard & Poor's Capital IQ, and Argus. However, you will need a subscription to access these platforms.

You can find less detailed summaries of analyst reports through summary sites, such as Yahoo Finance, Reuters, Zacks Investment Research, and NASDAQ.com.

There are three types of analyst reports:

- Initiating coverage reports are released when a firm starts covering a company for the first time. They provide information on company history, trends, and competitors

- Company analyst reports focus on the financial performance of the company, but also have some qualitative analysis

- Industry analyst reports have detailed analysis of an entire industry. They provide information on market sizes, shares, and major trends

What do I need to know?

We can categorize all of the information you need to know into objective and subjective information.

Objective information

Objective information is based on factual evidence. It does not require you to take a stance or have an opinion because this type of information is generally accepted to be true.

These are the major objective pieces of information you should know:

- What is the company's mission statement or aspiration?

- What are the company's products and services?

- What is the company's business model?

- Who are the company's customers?

- Who are the company's competitors?

The company's 10-K or other annual reports will have all of this information.

Subjective information

Subjective information is based on personal opinions, interpretations, and judgment. Subjective information can be found in online articles and analyst reports.

You should try to build a perspective of the company. You should have an opinion on how the company is doing, what they should be focusing on, and what their major challenges are.

A SWOT analysis is a helpful framework for conducting subjective research. SWOT stands for strengths, weaknesses, opportunities, and threats.

- **Strengths**: What does the company do well? What qualities differentiate them from competitors?

- **Weaknesses**: What does the company do poorly? What are the things that competitors do better?

- **Opportunities**: Where are the opportunities for growth or improvement?

- **Threats**: Who are the most threatening competitors? What are the major risks to the company's business?

If you can answer these questions, then you have a strong and well-defined perspective on the company.

In addition to researching the company, you should also research the specific role and team you are interviewing for. Speaking to current and former employees will be the most helpful for this.

Helpful questions to ask include:

- What are the responsibilities or tasks of the role?

- What skills or attributes are preferred or required?

- How does the role fit with the broader organization?

- What are the primary goals or targets of the team?

- What is the culture of the team and company like?

Example of company research

Let's take a look at an example of what completed company research looks like. We'll research the company LinkedIn for an upcoming PM interview.

LinkedIn Company Research

What is the company's mission statement or aspiration?

- *To connect the world's professionals to make them more productive and successful*

What are the company's products and services?

- *LinkedIn is a professional social media network*

- *LinkedIn has three main offerings that generate revenue: Talent Solutions, Marketing Solutions, and Premium subscriptions*

- *Talent Solutions represents ~65% of LinkedIn's revenue and consists of two parts. The first part helps recruiters attract, recruit, and hire talent. The second part, Learning Solutions, offers online courses to enterprise clients and individuals*

- *Marketing Solutions represents ~18% of LinkedIn's revenue. LinkedIn sells advertising and sponsored postings*

- *Premium subscriptions represent ~17% of LinkedIn's revenue. This offering allows users to increase their search results, send messages, contact members outside of their networks, and see information about people that have viewed their profile*

- *Premium subscriptions also include Sales Solutions, which enables users to generate quality leads to increase sales*

What is the company's business model?

- *LinkedIn operates a freemium business model*

- *LinkedIn attracts a large user base by making it free for anyone to join and use*

- *LinkedIn then makes money by selling premium offerings to a subset of customers that are willing to pay*

Who are the company's customers?

- *LinkedIn's free users are primarily working professionals*

- *For Talent Solutions, customers are recruiters and other human resources employees*

- *For Marketing Solutions, customers are advertising, marketing, and sales employees*

- *For Premium subscriptions, customers are job seekers, recruiters, and salespeople*

Who are the company's competitors?

- *In the social media market, major competitors include Facebook, Twitter, and Snapchat*

- *In the job search and recruiting market, major competitors include Indeed, Glassdoor, CareerBuilder, and ZipRecruiter*

- *In the advertising market, major competitors include Google, Facebook, and Microsoft*

- *In the online learning market, major competitors include Coursera, Khan Academy, Udemy, and Skillshare*

Strengths

- *Massive user base of over 600 million users, which is difficult to replicate*
- *Strong network effects; the value of LinkedIn to users increases as the number of users increases*
- *Diversified revenue streams coming from three different products*
- *Strong content business with articles and posts written by professional leaders and influencers around the world*
- *Tremendous amount of data on employees and companies to identify unmet needs*

Weaknesses

- *LinkedIn's users have much less engagement on the platform than other social networks*
- *Only 20% of users are paying customers*
- *LinkedIn's mix of premium offerings is confusing and unclear to many potential customers*
- *Allegations of the company's invasion of privacy have hurt LinkedIn's brand name*

Opportunities

- *Opportunity to further increase user base by targeting more blue-collar workers*
- *Opportunity to increase the percentage of paying users by improving the Premium subscription offering*
- *Opportunity to replace headhunting and recruiting companies if LinkedIn decides to enter the recruiting-as-a-service business*

- *Opportunity to increase user engagement on the platform to increase the value of its advertising business*

Threats

- *Other large social media platforms (e.g., Facebook) may eventually enter the job search and recruiting markets*
- *Smaller, niche professional networks (e.g., minority networks) may better meet a customer segment's needs*
- *Difficulty balancing the different needs of job seekers and recruiters when creating and selling premium offerings*
- *Challenges in managing more fraudulent and uncredible accounts as the user base grows*

What are the responsibilities or tasks of the role?

- *Work with cross-functional teams to build and launch products globally, from initial market validation, positioning and messaging, to go-to-market strategy and launch execution*
- *Own user and product insights to build data-driven, actionable insights that inform product strategy*

What skills or attributes are preferred or required?

- *Work autonomously, focusing on critical outcomes amidst competing priorities and tight deadlines*
- *Inspire and lead cross-functional teams*
- *Use market research to inform product development strategies*
- *Execute and scale high impact, multi-channel go-to-market efforts*

How does the role fit with the broader organization?

- *Work with data scientists, engineers, marketers, and salespeople to build and launch products*
- *Product managers are organized into product-specific and segment-specific teams*

What are the primary goals or targets of the team?

- *Increase customer engagement with the platform*
- *Increase customer monetization*

What is the culture of the team and company like?

- *A culture of people who want to change the world*
- *A transparent company with bi-weekly all-hands meetings in which the CEO gives updates and answers questions*
- *LinkedIn provides InDays each month to allow employees to focus on themselves, the company, and the world*
- *LinkedIn provides Speaker Series to expose employees to inspiring ideas and innovative thinkers from around the globe*

Summary

- Conducting company research before your interview can help you demonstrate interest in the company or role and speak intelligently when asked interview questions

- There are four major sources of information you should look into when conducting company research:

    - Company annual report

    - Online articles

    - Current and former employees

    - Analyst reports

- Essential information you should know about the company includes:

    - What is the company's mission statement or aspiration?

    - What are the company's products and services?

    - What is the company's business model?

    - Who are the company's customers?

    - Who are the company's competitors?

- Use a SWOT analysis to build a perspective on the company

    - **Strengths**: What does the company do well? What qualities differentiate them from competitors?

    - **Weaknesses**: What does the company do poorly? What are the things that competitors do better?

  - **Opportunities**: Where are the opportunities for growth or improvement?
  - **Threats**: Who are the most threatening competitors? What are the major risks to the company's business?

- You should also research the specific role and team you are interviewing for:
  - What are the responsibilities or tasks of the role?
  - What skills or attributes are preferred or required?
  - How does the role fit with the broader organization?
  - What are the primary goals or targets of the team?
  - What is the culture of the team and company like?

Practice

1. Conduct company research for a company that you are interviewing for.

3. Define Yourself Questions

What are define yourself questions?

Define yourself questions ask about your professional identity, including your skills, qualities, values, and goals.

These are open-ended questions that aim to understand who you are as a person, beyond the surface level information listed on your resume.

There are seven common questions you should be prepared for:

- Walk me through your resume
- What is your greatest strength?
- What is your greatest weakness?
- Where do you see yourself in 5-10 years?
- Why should we hire you?
- Why are you leaving your current job?

- What do you do in your free time?

What are interviewers looking for?

There are three main qualities interviewers are looking for:

- **Strong achievements**: Interviewers want to see that you've made significant achievements at school or in your professional career. Past performance can be an indicator for future success

- **Passion for product**: Interviewers want to see that you are enthusiastic, curious, and devoted to being a product manager. They are trying to hire someone that will stay in the role for the long-term

- **Personality and cultural fit**: Interviewers want to see that you would be a great fit with their team and company. Commonly desired attributes include being friendly, collaborative, coachable, and energetic

Walk me through your resume

The "walk me through your resume" question is most commonly asked at the beginning of the interview. You should prepare for it to make a great first impression with the interviewer.

In asking this question, interviewers are looking to learn two things.

One, they want to get a quick overview of your work experience and achievements. Often, interviewers don't have the time to look through your resume before the interview.

Two, they want to understand why you are suited for the role and why you are interested in working at the company. The "walk me through your resume" question is a quick way to assess this.

Therefore, in answering this question, follow this strategy:

- Start with a strong opening statement that summarizes your areas of expertise and number of years of experience
- Highlight your most relevant and impressive experiences and accomplishments, starting with the most recent
- Connect your experiences to why you're interested in the role and why you would be a good fit

Let's take a look at a few examples of how candidates walk interviewers through their resume.

***Example #1**: Walk me through your resume.*

I am a marketing and strategy professional with over seven years of experience in media and e-commerce.

I spent the last five years working at Activision Blizzard, where I led social media marketing. I planned and executed marketing campaigns that led to over $1 million in sales. I also developed a marketing strategy that lowered customer acquisition costs by 15%.

Before that, I spent two years working at LinkedIn in their ads team. I ran customer surveys and focus groups to identify key customer pain points for ad purchasers. From this, I launched over fifty tailored email campaigns that had a 25% higher conversion rate than previous campaigns.

Given my experience in data-driven marketing and strategy, I believe I would be an excellent fit for a product manager role at Amazon.

***Example #2**: Walk me through your resume.*

I am currently a management consultant at the Boston Consulting Group and have three years of experience working on a variety of strategic and operational projects.

On the strategy side, I advised a telecom client on potential adjacent markets to enter. This translated to an expected revenue growth of 20% per year over the next five years.

On the operations side, I helped an airline company identify over $200M in annual cost savings by adjusting their flight schedules and passenger capacity. I also worked with a utility company on a pricing strategy to increase incremental revenues by 15% per year.

These experiences have helped me build a strategic and operational toolkit. I believe this toolkit would make me an exceptional fit for tackling the challenging business problems at Adobe. I am passionate about using my skills to drive immediate, tangible impacts for Adobe and its customers.

***Example #3**: Walk me through your resume.*

I am a senior at Duke University, majoring in electrical and computer engineering with a passion for technology.

Last summer, I worked at IBM as a business development intern. I collaborated with over ten sales members to generate over $700K in potential sales leads.

Before that, I worked in a biology research lab that focuses on using machine learning to identify potential tumors from ultrasound images. I worked on a project to improve tumor identification algorithm accuracy by over 50% for select use cases.

I want to continue building on my work experiences and believe Google would be a great fit for me. I am excited about potentially working as a business analyst so that I can take on increased responsibilities and make a meaningful impact.

What is your greatest strength?

The "what is your greatest strength" question is asked for three main reasons.

One, interviewers want to see that you are humble and don't have an ego. How you answer this question will help the interviewer identify if you are grounded and down-to-earth. PMs work closely in teams, so many companies value this quality.

Two, interviewers want to see that you have strengths that are relevant to the PM role. Therefore, you should choose a strength that will greatly help you as a PM. Examples of great strengths to mention include:

- Prioritizing tasks based on their impact and performance
- Thinking creatively and innovatively when brainstorming ideas or solutions
- Responding to changing conditions or feedback flexibly and smoothly
- Collaborating effectively with teams across various departments
- Articulating ideas clearly and effectively to various stakeholders
- Using data and analytics effectively in making decisions
- Planning and executing a long-term vision or plan
- Understanding and empathizing with the needs and pain points of customers
- Navigating complex stakeholder relationships and driving alignment
- Influencing stakeholders and team members to gain buy-in
- Persevering through challenges and setbacks to achieve desired outcomes

- Managing time efficiently to meet deadlines and deliver high-quality work

Three, this question is another way for your interviewer to assess your communications skills. Can you communicate your strengths in a clear, concise way? Is your answer believable or credible?

You should structure your answer. A structure will help keep your answer concise, easy to follow, and focused. We recommend using the following structure:

- Provide a one sentence, high-level summary of your greatest strength

- Illustrate your strength with an example

- Explain how this strength will help you as a product manager

Example #1: *What is your greatest strength?*

My greatest strength is my analytical mindset and data-driven decision-making.

One example that highlights this strength is from my time at a fintech startup. I was tasked with optimizing the user onboarding process for a mobile app.

I conducted a thorough analysis of user behavior data, identified pain points in the onboarding flow, and recommended targeted improvements.

By A/B testing different onboarding sequences and iterating based on user feedback, I was able to increase the conversion rate by 25% within a month.

As I move towards a PM role, this strength will allow me to make informed decisions based on data and insights. By leveraging analytics, I can identify market trends, understand user behavior, and prioritize features that provide the most value to our customers. This will ultimately lead to the development of products that resonate with the target audience and drive business growth.

***Example #2**: What is your greatest strength?*

My greatest strength is my ability to effectively prioritize and manage cross-functional teams to deliver high-impact products on time and within budget.

For instance, in my previous role at Google, I was tasked with launching a critical feature within a tight deadline to meet a market opportunity.

I conducted a thorough assessment of the project's requirements, collaborated closely with engineering, design, and marketing teams, and established a clear roadmap with well-defined milestones.

By setting clear expectations and maintaining open lines of communication, we were able to streamline the development process and successfully launch the feature ahead of schedule, resulting in a 30% increase in user engagement.

I believe this strength is critical for a PM because it ensures that projects are executed efficiently and on time. By effectively managing priorities and resources, I believe I can make significant contributions towards the company's overall success.

What is your greatest weakness?

The "what is your greatest weakness?" question is asked for three main reasons.

One, interviewers want to see that you are humble and don't have an ego. Recognizing that you have a weakness will make you appear grounded and down-to-earth.

Two, this question is a test to see whether you have a growth mindset and are constantly working to improve yourself. PMs constantly look for development opportunities to grow their skillset.

Three, this question is another way for your interviewer to assess your communications skills. Can you communicate your weakness in a clear, concise way? Is your answer believable or credible?

For these reasons, it is important to take the time to craft your answer to the "what is your greatest weakness?" question carefully. You want to choose a weakness that will help you demonstrate these three qualities without raising any red flags to the interviewer.

Below are some examples of great weaknesses to talk about in your PM interview:

- Focusing too much on details and not enough on the big picture
- Difficulty presenting effectively in front of large groups
- Trouble working effectively with people that have different working styles
- Difficulty recognizing when to give up on an idea and move onto something else
- Trouble tackling ambiguous or unclear problems
- Slow decision-making when it comes to handling important or big problems
- Inability to fully consider other people's thoughts and feelings when making decisions
- Difficulty motivating oneself when team morale is low
- Trouble delegating work to others effectively
- Difficulty keeping track of all of the small, but important details
- Trouble motivating others during stressful or difficult times
- Trouble persuading and convincing others
- Trouble exhibiting confidence in front of others

- Inability to take calculated risks when necessary
- Difficulty standing up for oneself when challenged by others
- Trouble staying focused on one thing at a time

You should structure your answer. A structure will help keep your answer concise, easy to follow, and focused. We recommend using the following structure:

- Provide a one sentence, high-level summary of your greatest weakness
- Illustrate your weakness with an example
- Explain the specific steps you have taken to improve on this weakness
- Describe the tangible outcomes as a result of your improvement
- Reflect on your progress and what you have learned and what you have left to learn or practice

Providing a one sentence, high-level summary in the beginning of your answer will make the rest of your answer easier to follow. Illustrating your weakness with an example will make your answer more clear and credible.

The last three bullets in this structure help demonstrate that you are an introspective, action-oriented person. It shows that you actively track your progress and are excited to continue growing and improving.

Example #1: *What is your greatest weakness?*

My greatest weakness is that I tend to be overly self-critical, which can sometimes lead to a hesitation in decision-making.

For example, in my previous role as a business analyst at Target, I was often tasked with presenting findings and recommendations to the leadership team. Due to my tendency to overthink and second-guess myself, I would sometimes spend more time than necessary refining my presentations, which occasionally led to missed deadlines.

To address this, I've actively worked on building my confidence and trust in my abilities. I've started setting specific time limits for tasks like preparing presentations, allowing me to strike a balance between thoroughness and timeliness. Additionally, I've sought feedback from trusted colleagues and mentors to gain perspective on areas where I can be more assertive in my decision-making.

As a result of these efforts, I've noticed a significant improvement in my ability to make timely decisions without compromising quality. I've also received positive feedback from colleagues and supervisors on my increased efficiency in project delivery.

Reflecting on this progress, I've learned the importance of striking a balance between self-reflection and taking action. While being self-critical can lead to higher standards, it's crucial not to let it hinder progress. Moving forward, I plan to continue practicing decisiveness and seeking feedback to further refine this aspect of my professional approach.

***Example #2**: What is your greatest weakness?*

My greatest weakness is that I sometimes struggle with delegation, especially when I'm particularly invested in a project or goal.

For example, in my previous role, there was a project with a tight deadline that I was very passionate about. I found it challenging to delegate tasks to other team members, as I wanted to ensure that everything was executed to my exact vision and standards. This resulted in me taking on too much of the workload, which ultimately led to burnout and a loss in working efficiency.

I've been actively working on improving my delegation skills. I've started by identifying team members' strengths and assigning tasks accordingly, ensuring that each person is working on something that aligns with their expertise and experiences. Additionally, I've learned to provide clear instructions and set expectations, allowing me to trust in my team's capabilities more.

As a result, I've seen an improvement in my team's productivity and morale. By effectively delegating tasks, we've been able to meet deadlines more consistently and produce higher-quality work.

Reflecting on this learning experience, I've learned to appreciate the value of empowering team members and leveraging their strengths to achieve collective success. While it's important to be hands-on at times, it's equally important to trust and support the capabilities of the team.

Where do you see yourself in 5-10 years?

This question primarily assesses your passion for product. Do you plan to still be in a product-related role in 5-10 years?

This helps interviewers assess whether you are interested in product only for the short-term or for the long-term. Interviewers want to hire PMs that will ideally stay in the role for at least a few years.

Asking this question is an easy way for interviewers to get a sense for this.

Examples of good answers to give include:

- Continuing in product management, but taking an increasingly larger leadership role by leading larger teams and managing more products
- Exploring opportunities to start your own product-related venture, leveraging the skills and insights gained in product management
- Moving towards a product strategy role, working on shaping the overall product strategy of the entire company
- Driving product innovation by staying at the forefront of emerging technologies and evolving customer needs

- Becoming an industry expert and thought leader in product management that speaks at conferences and provides consulting to businesses

You should use the following structure when answering this question:

- Provide a one-sentence, high-level summary of the role or position you aspire towards
- Describe the impact you would make in this role or position
- Explain how the skills and insights you would gain in the current role you are interviewing for will help you in your career trajectory

Example #1: *Where do you see yourself in 5 years?*

In five years, I see myself in a leadership role as a more senior product manager, guiding and managing a larger cross-functional team and having increased responsibilities and impact.

I am eager to take on more responsibilities mentoring junior product managers and sharing my knowledge and expertise across a wider range of stakeholders. I find fulfillment in facilitating the professional growth of others.

I'm also eager to take on projects that are more complex and have a wider scope of impact. I enjoy seeing the tangible results of the projects that I work on.

The experiences and skills I would gain in this current role would serve as a strong foundation for my growth towards being a more senior product manager, allowing me to lead impactful product initiatives and contribute significantly to my team's and the company's overall success.

Example #2: *Where do you see yourself in 10 years?*

In 10 years, I aspire towards being a seasoned Product Director, leading a large, dynamic team to develop innovative solutions that will disrupt markets.

In this role, I would have the privilege of shaping the overall product strategy and roadmap and having a transformative impact on the organization's entire product portfolio.

What truly excites me about being a Product Director is the chance to foster a culture of innovation and excellence. I am passionate about creating an environment where team members are inspired to think creatively, take calculated risks, and push boundaries in pursuit of extraordinary product outcomes.

Through effective leadership and mentorship, I aim to empower my team to consistently deliver solutions that exceed customer expectations and disrupt markets.

I am eager to acquire the skills and insights in this current role so that I can have a solid foundation as I aspire towards this long-term career trajectory.

Why should we hire you?

The "why should we hire you?" question is a direct way for the interviewer to ask you why you are better than other candidates.

Many candidates do not prepare for this question and are surprised or caught off guard when interviewers ask this.

By taking the time to prepare for this question in advance, your answer will sound much more cohesive and impressive than the majority of answers.

You should use the following structure when answering this question:

- "You should hire me for the following three reasons"
- "One…" [Example]

- "Two..." [Example]
- "Three..." [Example]
- "For these reasons, I believe that I would be a great fit for the role and would be able to make an immediate, tangible impact on the company"

Example #1: *Why should we hire you?*

You should hire me for the following three reasons.

Firstly, I bring a strong analytical mindset to the table. In my previous role as a business analyst intern, I conducted market research that directly contributed to a 20% increase in customer acquisition. By synthesizing and analyzing data, I identified key customer segments and recommended targeted marketing strategies. This analytical rigor and track record of driving revenue growth through data-driven insights would be valuable in the product manager role.

Secondly, I am a highly adaptable and quick learner. During my internship, I immersed myself in diverse projects across various industries. In one instance, I successfully transitioned from analyzing consumer goods markets to the tech industry, contributing to a project that led to a 15% increase in market share for our client. This ability to swiftly grasp and apply new information is critical in the fast-paced environment of product management.

Lastly, I possess strong communication and collaboration skills. In my previous role, I consistently received positive feedback for my ability to convey complex findings in a clear and concise manner. My effective communication skills contributed to a 25% reduction in project completion times through improved coordination between departments. As a product manager, these skills are vital for leading teams, presenting product strategies, and fostering effective collaboration.

For these reasons, I believe I would be a great fit for the role and would be able to make an immediate, tangible impact on the company. My analytical mindset, adaptability, and communication skills would allow me to effectively drive product development, collaborate with cross-functional teams, and deliver solutions that meet both customer needs and business objectives.

Example #2: *Why should we hire you?*

You should consider hiring me for the following three reasons.

One, I have strong problem solving abilities. In my previous role as a project coordinator, I identified bottlenecks in workflows and implemented process improvements that drove a 25% improvement in operational efficiency.

Two, I possess a keen eye for user experience design. For a web application I collaborated on, I conducted user research and went through an iterative process to create an intuitive and user-friendly interface that resulted in a 20% increase in customer satisfaction.

Three, I believe I have strong leadership skills. I previously led a cross-functional team in a product launch that resulted in a successful go-to-market strategy and a 30% increase in product adoption. I effectively motivated and guided team members, ensuring alignment with project objectives and milestones.

For these reasons, I believe I would bring a unique combination of strengths to the role that would enable me to make a significant impact on the company.

Why are you leaving your current job?

By asking this question, interviewers are trying to understand the motivations behind the changes in your professional history. Interviewers want to see if the decision to leave your previous job is driven by a desire for growth and new challenges, or if there are any potential red flags.

When answering this question, it is important that you answer it in a positive tone. Avoid speaking negatively about your current or previous employer.

You should try to emphasize professional growth as the main reason for leaving your current job. You could say:

- You are looking for an opportunity to take on more responsibilities
- You are looking for an opportunity to move into a leadership role
- You are trying to diversify your skill set and learn new skills
- You are looking for new challenges

Other valid reasons that you could give include:

- Your current company went through restructuring, which impacted your role or growth opportunities
- You have a personal or family-related reason that requires relocation

Example: *Why are you leaving your current job?*

I've thoroughly enjoyed my time at my current company, where I've had the privilege of spearheading the development of a groundbreaking product in the retail space.

However, as the project reaches its maturity, I am looking for a new challenge because I feel like there is not much more I can learn in my current role.

I've been working on a product in the retail space for so many years, so am looking to work on an exciting, new project in a different industry or market. Technology has been an industry that has always interested me, so I'm drawn to your company because many of your products are at the forefront of technological innovation and design.

Additionally, the current team I am working on is quite small. I'm looking for a role or opportunity where I can work with a larger, more cross-functional team.

What do you do in your free time?

While this question may sound very casual, your answer actually gives the interviewer a lot of insights into your character, interests, and ability to maintain a healthy work-life balance.

In asking this question, interviewers want to see that you have a fulfilling and meaningful life outside of work. They want to see that you are motivated and social.

When answering this question, it is important that you are authentic. Do not lie and make up specific hobbies or interests just because you think that is what the interviewers want to hear.

For example, if you say that in your free time you read news on the latest technology products, attend product manager conferences or seminars, take online classes on leadership, and practice giving speeches in front of large audiences, the interviewer will most likely not believe you.

Instead, strike a balance between personal and professional interests.

There are a number of meaningful things you could mention:

- Spending time with family
- Playing with your pets
- Pursuing recreational hobbies
- Getting involved with your community
- Working on a side project or side business
- Learning and developing specific professional skills

Additionally, regardless of what you decide to say, make sure to emphasize continuous learning and growth. You want to demonstrate that you are committed to learning and personal development.

Example: *What do you do in your free time?*

In my free time, I prioritize a healthy work-life balance by engaging in a mix of personal and professional activities. Spending quality time with my family and my dog is a priority for me. It helps me recharge from a long day at work.

I'm an avid photographer. Photography allows me to explore my creative side and learn new skills. I've recently been trying to get better at taking action shots.

I also volunteer at a local animal adoption center, helping manage and organize volunteer shifts.

Lastly, I have a small travel blog. I document my experiences traveling to different countries to help others plan their vacations more easily.

Summary

- Define yourself questions ask about your professional identity, including your skills, qualities, values, and goals

- How to answer "Walk me through your resume"

    - Start with a strong opening statement that summarizes your areas of expertise and number of years of experience

    - Highlight your most relevant and impressive experiences and accomplishments, starting with the most recent

    - Connect your experiences to why you're interested in the role and why you would be a good fit

- How to answer "What is your greatest strength?"

    - Provide a one sentence, high-level summary of your greatest strength

    - Illustrate your strength with an example

    - Explain how this strength will help you as a product manager

- How to answer "What is your greatest weakness?"

    - Provide a one sentence, high-level summary of your greatest weakness

    - Illustrate your weakness with an example

    - Explain the specific steps you have taken to improve on this weakness

    - Describe the tangible outcomes as a result of your improvement

  - Reflect on your progress and what you have learned and what you have left to learn or practice

- How to answer "Where do you see yourself in 5-10 years?"

  - Provide a one sentence, high-level summary of the role or position you aspire towards

  - Describe the impact you would make in this role or position

  - Explain how the skills and insights you would gain in the current role you are interviewing for will help you in your career trajectory

- How to answer "Why should we hire you?"

  - "You should hire me for the following three reasons"

  - "One…" [Example]

  - "Two…" [Example]

  - "Three…" [Example]

  - "For these reasons, I believe that I would be a great fit for the role and would be able to make an immediate, tangible impact on the company"

- How to answer "Why are you leaving your current job?"

  - Answer in a positive tone; avoid speaking negatively about your current or previous employer

  - Emphasize professional growth as the main reason for leaving your current job

- How to answer "What do you do in your free time?"

- Give an authentic answer; do not make up specific hobbies or interests because you think that is what the interviewers want to hear

- Strike a balance between personal and professional interests

- Emphasize continuous learning and growth

Practice

1. Walk me through your resume.
2. What is your greatest strength?
3. What is your greatest weakness?
4. Where do you see yourself in ten years?
5. Why should we hire you?
6. Why are you leaving your current job?
7. What do you do in your free time?

4. Motivational Questions

What are motivational questions?

You are almost certainly going to be asked at least one motivational question at some point during your PM interviews.

Motivational questions ask you to explain your interests, passions, and goals.

There are two different motivational questions you should prepare for:

1. Why are you interested in product management?
2. Why do you want to work at this company?

What are interviewers looking for?

Interviewers primarily ask motivational questions for three reasons.

One, interviewers want to assess how interested and passionate you are about the job. Conducting interviews is an extremely time-consuming process. So, interviewers want to be able to quickly filter out people that are not interested in the job.

By asking motivational questions, interviewers can quickly narrow down the candidate pool to those that are likely to accept the job offer. Interviewers can also get a sense of who is likely to stay in the role for a longer period of time.

Two, interviewers can assess whether your interests align with the missions and values of the company. If what you are looking for does not align with the company or role, then you are likely a poor fit.

Three, motivational questions assess how well candidates can communicate. Does the candidate explain their interests and motivations clearly and articulately? Does the candidate keep their answers concise?

Even if you are genuinely passionate about the job and are a good fit for the role, poor communication will make it difficult for the interviewer to see this.

Taking these things into account, focus on demonstrating the following three qualities:

- Express genuine and credible interest and passion
- Demonstrate cultural fit with the firm
- Communicate clearly, concisely, and confidently

Let's walk through each of the different motivational questions to understand how to best answer each.

Why are you interested in product management?

There are many different reasons you could give for why you are interested in product management. Identify three compelling reasons for your answer.

Your reasons should focus on the responsibilities and potential impact of being a PM

In other words, what parts of the product management job make you excited? What responsibilities of product management make you feel fulfilled? What kind of impact are you looking to make?

Use the following simple, but effective structure when answering this question:

- "I am interested in product management for three reasons"
- "One..."
- "Two..."
- "Three..."
- "Given these interests, I believe product management is the perfect fit"

Reasons you could give for why you are interested in product management include:

- You like collaborating with cross-functional teams, which makes work more dynamic and interesting
- You value the high level of autonomy and responsibility that PM affords you through acting as a mini-CEO of a product
- You are excited about the potential impact you can make as a product manager, influencing how thousands or millions of people will use a product
- You love solving complex problems that are intellectually stimulating and rewarding
- You enjoy having the opportunity to create something new and innovative, shaping the direction of a product from its features to its user experience

- You find excitement in analyzing data to find insights to make tough product decisions
- You enjoy the customer-centricity of being a PM, helping create products that genuinely improve people's lives
- You value the professional growth and development that comes from the challenges and responsibilities of being a PM

Let's look at examples of how you could answer this question.

Example #1: *Why are you interested in product management?*

I'm interested in product management for three reasons.

One, I find fulfillment in having tremendous responsibility and ownership over a product or part of a product. This responsibility motivates me to work hard and makes me excited about work.

Two, I enjoy the cross-functional nature of the role. I like collaborating with different teams and get energy from working with a diverse group of people.

Three, I am excited to see the real and tangible impact that I make from my work. I get fulfillment from not only setting the product strategy and roadmap but seeing the product strategy and roadmap through to execution and implementation.

Given these interests, I believe product management is the perfect fit for me.

Example #2: *Why are you interested in product management?*

There are three reasons why I'm interested in product management.

Firstly, I am excited about the opportunity to shape products from ideation to launch. Working on every stage of a product's development is incredibly appealing to me. I appreciate the tremendous ownership of having end-to-end involvement and am excited to see the tangible impact of my work.

Secondly, I thrive on problem solving and enjoy the dynamic nature of product management. PM requires the ability to navigate a variety of challenges, from prioritizing features to aligning cross-functional teams. This dynamic environment excites me and aligns with my strengths and interests.

Thirdly, I'm drawn to the customer focus aspect of product management. Understanding and meeting the needs of the end-users is at the heart of every successful product. I find it incredibly rewarding to conduct user research, gather feedback, and translate it into actionable insights that drive product improvements.

For these reasons, I believe product management is the perfect fit for me.

Why do you want to work at this company?

There are also many reasons you could give for why you are interested in working at a particular company. Identify three compelling reasons for your answer.

Use the following simple, but effective structure when answering this question:

- "[Company Name] is a top choice for me for three reasons"
- "One…"
- "Two…"
- "Three…"
- "For these reasons, I would love to work for [Company Name]"

If the company is truly your number one choice, make sure to state that in the first sentence. This goes a long way in demonstrating your interest in the job. If the company is not your number one choice, just say that the company is a top choice for you.

Additionally, if the company has a strong mission or core value that employees strongly believe in, you should mention the mission or values of the company in your answer.

Otherwise, select the three reasons that are the most compelling and credible.

Reasons you could give for why you are interested in working at a particular company include:

- The company has deep expertise in a particular area or is at the forefront of innovation in an area you are interested in
- The company is a leader in the industry and you want to learn from the best
- You believe strongly in the company's missions and values and want to be a part of that
- You enjoy using the company's products or services
- You've loved the people that you met from the company and would like to work with them
- The company has a culture that is fun or empowering
- The company makes substantial investments in mentorship and personal development, which you value tremendously
- The company is at an exciting stage of growth or turnaround and you are excited about the opportunity to make an impact
- Several mentors that you respect and look up to have worked at the company and recommended working there

Let's look at a few examples of how to answer this question.

***Example #1**: Why do you want to work at LinkedIn?*

LinkedIn is my top choice company to work at. There are three reasons why I'm excited about LinkedIn.

One, I am passionate about LinkedIn's mission of creating economic opportunity. Throughout my career, I have found tremendous fulfillment in mentoring and coaching others in their professional development. I would love to further this passion by working at a company that focuses on connecting professionals and making them more productive and successful.

Two, I appreciate LinkedIn's strong company culture. Everyone that I have talked to at LinkedIn emphasizes how all of the employees are friendly, supportive, and hardworking. There is an expectation of taking ownership and making a real difference. I feel that I would thrive in this type of working culture.

Three, LinkedIn makes serious investments in employee development through various training programs and mentorship. I value professional development tremendously because I always want to learn new things and get better at what I do.

For these reasons, I would love to work at LinkedIn.

Example #2. *Why do you want to work at Netflix?*

Netflix is a top choice for me for three reasons.

One, I am excited about the potential career advancement at Netflix. Unlike many other companies, Netflix has a very transparent and structured promotion process and operates like a meritocracy. I value the potential promotion opportunities.

Two, the people that I've met that work at Netflix are among the smartest people I know. Everyone that I have met has had a very impressive background and list of achievements. I am excited to be potentially working with these people because I know I will learn a lot from them.

Three, I love using Netflix. It is something I use every day that brings great entertainment and joy in my life. I'd love to work for a company in which I use their product every day.

For these reasons, I am excited to have the opportunity to interview for such a great company.

Example #3: *Why do you want to work at Instacart?*

There are three primary reasons why I'm excited about Instacart.

One, I believe that Instacart is going through an exciting time of rapid growth, with new cities being added daily. I want to be a part of this process to learn how companies can grow so quickly and successfully.

Two, I am excited about the potential impact I can make at Instacart, which has the potential to touch over 80% of U.S. households. I want to improve the grocery shopping process for families, saving them time and money.

Three, I have enjoyed everyone that I have met from Instacart. They have been incredibly supportive in taking the time to answer my questions and in encouraging me to apply. I would love to work alongside these people.

For these reasons, I am very interested in working at Instacart.

Summary

Motivational questions

- The two motivational questions you should prepare for are:
  - Why are you interested in product management?
  - Why do you want to work at this company?
- Focus on demonstrating the following three qualities when answering these questions
  - Express genuine and credible interest and passion
  - Demonstrate cultural fit with the firm
  - Communicate clearly, concisely, and confidently

Why are you interested in product management?

- Use the structure: "I am interested in product management for three reasons. One… Two… Three… Given these interests, I believe product management is the perfect fit"
- Your reasons should focus on the responsibilities and the potential impact of being a PM

Why do you want to work at this company?

- Use the structure: "[Company Name] is a top choice for me for three reasons. One… Two… Three… For these reasons, I would love to work for [Company Name]"
- If the company is truly your number one choice, make sure to state it in your first sentence
- If the company has a strong mission or core value, ensure you mention it in your answer

Practice

1. Why are you interested in product management?
2. Select a company that you are interviewing for. Why do you want to work at that company?

5. Behavioral Questions

What are behavioral questions?

Behavioral questions, also known as fit questions, ask you to draw upon an experience in the past in which you demonstrated a particular skill or quality.

These types of questions are a way for interviewers to dive deeper beyond what is listed on your resume. It allows interviewers to understand you better on a deeper, more personal level.

Examples of behavioral questions include the following:

- Tell me about a time when you used data to solve a problem
- Give a time when you disagreed with your manager
- Describe a situation in which you handled conflict while working on a team
- Give an example of a time when you went above and beyond
- Tell me about a time when you failed

What are interviewers looking for?

Behavioral questions assess three things.

First, behavioral questions use past behavior to determine future performance or success. Since the candidate draws upon previous experiences and actions they have taken, interviewers can get a sense of how the candidate would perform on the job.

Second, these questions can reveal a candidate's personality and cultural fit with the firm. In answering behavioral questions, candidates show characteristics, such as being confident, humble, friendly, or collaborative. Candidates can also reveal the values and morals that they believe in.

Third, behavioral questions assess how well candidates can communicate. Does the candidate explain their experiences clearly and articulately? Does the candidate keep their stories concise?

Taking these three things into account, focus on demonstrating the following three qualities:

- Show evidence of impressive, tangible accomplishments
- Demonstrate personality and cultural fit with the firm
- Communicate clearly, concisely, and confidently

You can show evidence of impressive, tangible accomplishments by quantifying your accomplishments and explaining the impact of your work.

Don't just explain what you did and how you did it. Explain the impact and effect you had on the organization. What was the magnitude of the impact? How many people were affected? How did this impact annual revenues or costs?

Example: *Don't just say that you worked with others to analyze survey responses to identify customer improvement areas. Instead, say that you led* *an eight-person analytics team to analyze over 100K survey responses to identify improvement initiatives worth $200M in annual revenue.*

You can demonstrate personality and cultural fit with the firm by first understanding the firm's culture and values. Then, you can weave in these ideals and values into your answer.

Example: *If the company values collaboration, focus on drawing upon experiences in which you worked on a team or with multiple teams. If the company values innovation, focus on drawing upon experiences in which you changed the status quo.*

Finally, you can communicate clearly, concisely, and confidently by preparing your answers beforehand and practicing delivering them out loud.

The more behavioral questions you practice answering, the better you will get at telling stories about your past experiences. You will stumble less often when speaking and sound more confident.

How do you answer behavioral questions?

There are hundreds of different behavioral questions you could get asked. Preparing specific answers for each potential behavioral question is not practical or feasible. Instead, we recommend an alternative approach that is much more efficient and effective.

1. Prepare 6 - 8 different stories drawn upon your past professional and personal experiences. Select experiences that are the most impressive, impactful, or unique.

2. Ensure that your stories are collectively diverse. For example, you don't want to have eight stories all about leadership. Instead, have at least one story for leadership, teamwork, problem solving, resilience, integrity, decision making, communication, and interpersonal skills.

3. When asked a behavioral question, mentally run through your list of prepared stories and select the story that is the most relevant.

4. Adapt, reframe, or tailor your story to ensure that it emphasizes and focuses on the theme that the specific behavioral question is asking for.

5. When you get asked another behavioral question, mentally run through your prepared list of stories and select the story that is the most relevant that you have not shared yet.

This strategy for behavioral questions has three main advantages.

One, it is an efficient strategy to use because you only need to prepare 6 - 8 stories instead of hundreds of stories for the hundreds of potential behavioral questions.

Two, this strategy ensures that your mind will not go blank during an interview. You will be doing very minimal thinking on the spot because you will always have a prepared list of stories to share.

Three, this strategy ensures that you are sharing only the most impressive, impactful, or unique experiences. These stories are the ones that best highlight your traits and accomplishments.

Next, we'll discuss the best way to structure your stories.

Structuring your answers to behavioral questions is crucial because it keeps your stories concise and helps you focus on the key messages that you want to deliver.

90% of candidates use the STAR method to structure their answers for behavioral and fit interview questions. STAR stands for Situation, Task, Action, and Result.

While this structure definitely works, we recommend a different structure that is more clear, more concise, and will help make your answer stand out from the 90% of other candidates using the STAR method.

The method we've developed is called the SPAR method, which stands for Summary, Problem, Action, and Result.

When telling a story, go through each of these points.

1. Summary

Provide a one-sentence summary of the story that you are about to tell the interviewer. This helps make the rest of your story and answer easier to follow because the interviewer already knows the "what." They then can pay more attention to the "how" when you give your answer.

Example: *I'm going to share with you a story where I helped save Airbnb $10M per year by analyzing customer data and collaborating with cross-functional teams.*

2. Problem

Describe the problem you encountered or were asked to solve. Try to keep this section concise to spend more time on the Action and Results section.

You may want to answer the following questions:

- What were you asked to do?
- What was the goal or objective?
- Why was this task important?

Example: *While working at Airbnb in their strategic planning & analysis group, I had to determine whether the incremental $10M that Airbnb spent on initiatives to improve customer satisfaction had a positive return on investment. This was important because Airbnb was focused on cutting unnecessary costs to achieve better profitability.*

3. Action

Explain what steps you took to handle the task or meet the goal or objective. Make sure that the actions center around what you specifically did. Do not focus too much on speaking to what your team did because it takes away from your accomplishments.

You may want to answer the following questions:

- What steps did you take?
- How did you take these steps?
- Why did you take these actions?

Example: *I used SQL and Excel to analyze over 700K customer data points to create a model forecasting how much happy customers spend per year versus unhappy customers.*

I collaborated with data science, customer experience, and finance teams and persuaded them to give me their support and buy-in. I also performed competitor and industry benchmarking to validate the results further.

4. Result

Describe the outcome that your actions had, quantifying the impact and effect you had on the organization. Additionally, you can describe your key takeaways from this experience and how it impacted or influenced you as a person.

You may want to answer the following questions:

- Did you meet the goals or objectives?
- What was the outcome and impact of your actions?
- What did you learn from this experience?
- How did this experience help you grow and develop?

Example: *In the end, I determined that the customer satisfaction initiatives had a negative 20% return on investment. I presented the findings to the CFO and to my 30-person strategic planning & analysis group, who all supported my recommendation. My work would save Airbnb $10M per year moving forward.*

Throughout this process, I learned how to work with multiple cross-functional teams and how to persuade stakeholders to get their buy-in. This experience also further reinforced my perspective on using data to make intelligent business decisions.

What behavioral questions could I get asked?

Now that you know an efficient strategy to answer any behavioral question, you should become familiar with all of the different types of behavioral questions you could get asked.

Below is a list of fifty different behavioral and fit questions. This is not meant to be a comprehensive list of all questions, but the list will provide you with a clear idea of the different categories of behavioral questions.

Leadership questions

- Give me an example of a time when you had to lead a team
- Tell me about a time when you took on a leadership role
- Describe a situation in which you had to motivate someone
- Tell me about a time when you showed initiative
- Give me an example of a time when you went above and beyond the call of duty
- Tell me about a time when you had to be adaptable

- Share an example of a time when you had to lead a cross-functional team or collaborate with colleagues from different departments

Teamwork questions

- Describe a time when you had to make an individual sacrifice for the good of the team
- Tell me about a time when you worked on a highly effective team. What made the team so successful?
- Give an example of a time when you were part of a team that did not work well together. What were the reasons for this?
- Share an example that illustrates the typical role that you take on a team
- Can you tell me about your most recent experience working with a team?
- Give me a time when a team member wasn't doing their work. What did you do?
- Tell me about a time when you had to adapt to unexpected changes or challenges as a team

Problem solving questions

- Tell me about a time when you used data to solve a problem
- Describe a difficult or complicated problem that you faced. How did you approach the problem?
- Tell me about a time when you had to make a decision but did not have all of the information you needed
- Describe a time when you had too many things to do. How did you handle this?

- Give an example of a problem you solved in a unique way
- Share an example of a situation where you had to work with limited resources to achieve a goal

Resilience questions

- Describe a situation in which you handled conflict while working on a team
- Give an example of a time when you tried to accomplish something but failed
- Describe a situation in which you made a mistake. What did you do about it?
- Tell me about a time you failed to meet a deadline. What things did you do to fail? What did you learn?
- Give an example of a time when you had too many things to do. How did you handle this?
- Talk about a setback you had at work. What did you do?

Integrity questions

- Talk about a time when it was challenging to be honest
- Tell me about a time when you found out a colleague was doing something wrong. What did you do?
- Can you give me a situation in which you thought it was better to be dishonest?
- Describe a time when you followed a rule that you didn't agree with
- Can you describe a time when a colleague questioned your honesty? What did you do?

- Describe a time when you had to deliver difficult news or information to a colleague, client, or supervisor

Decision making questions

- Walk me through the steps you took to make an important decision you made at work
- Tell me about a time when you had to make an immediate decision without having all the information you need
- Give me an example of a time when you made a decision that wasn't popular
- Describe a decision that you regretted making. Why did you regret it?
- Give me a time when you had to make a difficult decision
- Describe a time when you had to make a decision that required you to take a calculated risk

Communication questions

- Describe a time when you had to give a presentation without any preparation
- Talk about a time when your communication failed. What was the problem? How did you handle it?
- Share an example of how you communicated with one of your previous bosses
- Give me an example of a time when you gave a speech or presentation for your job
- Tell me about a time when you communicated with an unresponsive person

- Describe a time when you had to adjust your communication style to effectively interact with a person with different communication preferences or cultural backgrounds

Interpersonal skills questions

- Give a time when you disagreed with your manager
- Describe a time you disagreed with a teammate
- Tell me about a time when you had to persuade someone on a particular course of action
- Give an example of a time when you mentored someone
- How have you maintained relationships with your former managers and coworkers?
- Was there ever a time you didn't get along with a colleague? What did you do?

Examples of answers to behavioral questions

***Example #1**: Describe a time when you went above and beyond the call of duty.*

While working at Apple in their AppleCare business, I was responsible for analyzing data to identify opportunities to improve customer satisfaction.

While looking through survey responses, I realized there was an opportunity to use the tremendous amount of data that Apple had to predict which customers were likely to cancel their AppleCare subscriptions.

Apple could focus on retaining these customers by sending them discount codes for renewal. I raised this point to my director and proposed taking on this project.

Outside of my regular job responsibilities, I pulled over five years of purchasing data for over 10 million customers to create a logistic regression model. I verified my model with data scientists and got the buy-in of members of the AppleCare strategy team.

In the end, I determined that Apple could increase revenues by $100M by targeting the top 10% of customers that were most likely to cancel and sending them discount codes.

I presented my results to the head of AppleCare, who approved testing this promotional campaign to a few cities. My director was appreciative of me going above and beyond what was required in my role.

***Example #2**: Describe a time when you had to motivate someone.*

While working on a customer service improvement project for Amazon, I led a four-person analytics team. The goal was to analyze recent customer survey data to identify ways to improve customer service.

I distributed work according to each person's interests and expertise. After a few weeks, I observed that three members worked productively and effectively while one member, John, was consistently delivering work that was both low-quality and late.

Realizing that this was a potential motivation issue, I sat down with John to understand what the root cause was. The problem was that the analytics team had recently shifted to using an analytics software called Tableau.

John found Tableau difficult to set up and use, so he was unmotivated to switch from using Excel, which he was an expert at. As a result, Excel could not handle the millions of rows of data, causing poor work quality and delays.

To motivate John, I set up three one-on-one Tableau training sessions with him to walk him through the setup of Tableau. I demonstrated how it could save him time because it performed computationally intensive calculations much quicker than Excel.

Afterward, John began liking Tableau. He became excited to learn about what other features of Tableau could save him time in his other projects. His performance significantly improved and he began consistently delivering high-quality work on-time.

Example #3: *Can you talk about a time when it was challenging to be honest?*

On my last project, I worked with a newly hired manager that was difficult to work with. He had an investment banking background and liked to overwork his team without taking breaks. We often would be expected to skip lunch to deliver work on-time.

The three other members of the team and I were miserable for the first two weeks working with him. After two weeks, the manager asked his direct reports for feedback on how things were going.

The three other members of the team were fearful of providing harsh feedback to the manager. Promotions were coming up in a few months and an unhappy manager could potentially write poor performance reviews for the team.

During my feedback session with the manager, I found it difficult to be honest in saying how things were going. However, I took a risk and decided to be honest. I explained that I felt that his working style was not a good fit for the team.

I explained that it was unhealthy to skip meals and that this made the team hungry, unhappy, and unproductive. I asked if we could be more thoughtful in prioritizing work and reducing the amount of time spent working on tasks that were not critically important. I also proposed scheduling breaks for the team to relax together, which could improve productivity later.

The manager was surprisingly receptive to the feedback. He explained that this was his first corporate role and that he was still adjusting to the company culture and expectations.

As a result, the manager took my suggestions. The team immediately became happier and more motivated. We completed the project on-time without working any weekends by focusing on the most important tasks.

Summary

- Behavioral questions, also known as fit questions, ask you to draw upon an experience in the past in which you demonstrated a particular skill or quality

- Focus on demonstrating the following three qualities when answering behavioral questions:

    - Show evidence of impressive, tangible accomplishments

    - Communicate clearly, concisely, and confidently

    - Demonstrate your personality and cultural fit with the firm

- Prepare 6 – 8 different stories drawn upon your past professional and personal experiences

- Ensure that your stories are collectively diverse and cover a variety of different themes, such as: leadership, teamwork, problem solving, resilience, integrity, decision making, communication, and interpersonal skills

- When asked a behavioral question, mentally run through your prepared list of stories and select the one that is the most relevant that you have not shared yet

- Structure your answer using the SPAR method

    - **Summary**: Provide a one-sentence summary of the story that you are about to tell the interviewer

    - **Problem**: Describe the problem you encountered or were asked to solve

    - **Action**: Explain what steps you took to handle the task or to meet the goal or objective

- **Result**: Describe the outcome that your actions had, quantifying the impact and effect you had on the organization

Practice

1. Tell me about a time when you used data to solve a problem.
2. Describe a situation in which you handled conflict while working on a team.
3. Give an example of a time when you tried to accomplish something, but failed.
4. Tell me about a time when you had to make a difficult decision.
5. Describe a time when you had to make an individual sacrifice for the good of the team.
6. Give me an example of a time when you had to lead a team.
7. Describe a time when you followed a rule that you didn't agree with.
8. Talk about a time when your communication failed. What was the problem? How did you handle it?

6. Product Questions

What are product questions?

Product questions ask you to discuss a product, including why you like it, dislike it, and how you would improve it. These questions assess your product knowledge and acumen.

These questions are predictive of how you would perform as a product manager. It gives the interviewer insights into how you think about and approach product.

There are three common product questions you should prepare for:

- What is your favorite product and why?
- What is your least favorite product and why?
- How would you design or improve a particular product?

What are interviewers looking for?

Interviewers are assessing four major skills and qualities when asking product questions:

- **Product knowledge**: Deep understanding of product features, functionalities, and how they address user needs and pain points
- **Customer focus**: Deep understanding of customer needs, preferences, and pain points
- **Creativity and innovation**: Ability to think outside of the box to generate new, exciting ideas
- **Structured, logical thinking**: Ability to methodically analyze problems, develop solutions, and evaluate potential outcomes

What is your favorite product and why?

The "what is your favorite product?" question is the most commonly asked product question in PM interviews.

You should expect to be asked this question at least once for each company or role that you apply for.

Given that you can prepare for this question in advance, this is an easy opportunity for you to deliver an outstanding, prepared answer and leave a positive first impression on your interviewers.

What product should I pick?

Picking the right product is critical in order to answer this question effectively and demonstrate your product knowledge.

Although you are free to pick any product that you want, we recommend that you pick a product that adheres to the following five principles:

1. The product is one that you know well

The easiest way to fail the "what is your favorite product?" question is to pick a product that you are not familiar with.

After you give your answer, the interviewer will likely dive deeper into your answer, asking you specific follow-up questions and potentially asking you to compare the product's specific features to other products.

If you do not know the product well, you will have a hard time answering these specific and detailed follow-up questions.

So, make sure you know the product very well. Ideally, you should:

- Know all of the pain points the product solves
- Know all of the different product features and specifications
- Know what are alternatives and substitutes for the product
- Have actually used the product, ideally several times

2. The product is complex enough

You should pick a product that is complex enough to have a meaningful conversation or discussion. This allows you to demonstrate your full product knowledge and acumen.

Picking a product that is too simple will make it difficult for the interviewer to have a more detailed or nuanced conversation with you.

3. The product is not ubiquitous

To help yourself stand out in PM interviews, you should ideally pick a product that is not super common. In other words, you don't want to give the same answer that thousands of other candidates give.

For example, many candidates will say that their favorite product is their smartphone. While you can form a great answer with this product, more often than not, your answer will be similar to answers that other candidates give.

4. The product is not too obscure or niche

You should not pick a product that is so obscure or niche that no one has ever heard of it.

If your interviewer is unfamiliar with the product, you'll have to spend time explaining the product to them. This can waste valuable time during the interview, giving yourself less time to explain why the product is your favorite.

Picking an obscure or extremely niche product also makes it harder for the interviewer to have a productive discussion with you on its features or specifications.

5. The product is relevant to the company

Ideally, your product should be somewhat relevant to the company. It does not need to be in the same industry or have the same customers, but the product should be a similar type.

For example, if you are interviewing for a company that sells software. It may be beneficial to pick a favorite product that is also software. This way, you can demonstrate your knowledge and acumen of software products.

In this example, if you had picked a physical product, such as furniture or gym equipment, the type of product knowledge you demonstrate will be less relevant to the company.

What features or characteristics make a product great?

There are many different qualities that can make a product great. These include:

- **Ease of use**: The product is easy to set up and learn. It is intuitive and user friendly.
- **Reliability or stability**: The product can be depended on. It is consistent and repeatedly delivers the same results
- **Strong community or user base**: The product has a large or tight-knit community of users that help each other or make the product experience better for everyone
- **Flexibility**: The product can be used for a variety of different use cases or scenarios
- **Customizability**: The product can be easily modified or adapted to fit a user's specific needs or preferences
- **Scalability**: The use of the product can be easily increased or decreased to meet the needs of a growing or shrinking customer base
- **Innovation**: The product provides a new or fresh way of solving pain points or addressing needs
- **Integration**: The product can be used in conjunction with many other products easily and seamlessly
- **Compliance**: The product makes it easy to follow government regulations or laws
- **Affordability**: The product is priced lower than other products or has a pricing model that is more favorable for users

These are all great characteristics to look for when selecting a product that you like.

How should I structure my answer?

You should structure your answer to make it clearer and more concise for the interviewer to digest. You can use the following simple, but effective structure:

- "[Product] is my favorite product"
- "[1-2 sentence summary of what the product does]"
- "There are three reasons why this product is my favorite: [reason 1], [reason 2], [reason 3]"
- "[Reason 1]…"
- "[Reason 2]…"
- "[Reason 3]…"
- "For these reasons, I believe this product stands out compared to its alternatives and substitutes"

When giving the different reasons why a product is your favorite, the most important thing is to make sure your reasons are specific.

For example, don't just say that a product is easy to use.

Explain why the product is easy to use. What features or specifications make the product easy to use? Why do these features or specifications make it easy to use? Why is this important to the user? What pain points do these features or specifications address? How is this better than alternative or substitute products?

By making your reasons specific, you should naturally be able to incorporate your perspective on customer pain points and competing products. This will help you demonstrate that you have a comprehensive perspective of the product.

***Example #1**: What is your favorite product and why?*

My favorite product is Lyft Bikes. It is a bikeshare infrastructure in major cities that enables users to rent a bike for a short period of time to get from point A to point B.

There are three reasons why this product is my favorite: it addresses an unmet pain point of public and private transportation, it is easy for new users to use, and is convenient.

Living in a major city, there are often places that I need to go to that are too far to walk. Taking public buses is not an ideal option if there are no routes or stops near my destination. Taking a taxi or Uber is not an ideal option because they are expensive and are also susceptible to being stuck in traffic. Lyft Bikes solves this pain point because it can take me exactly where I want to go, more affordably than a taxi or Uber and also avoids road traffic.

Lyft Bikes is extremely easy to sign up for. As long as a user has the Lyft app, it takes a simple swipe to switch to the Lyft Bikes screen. Renting a bike takes a few seconds, you just need to scan a QR code on the bike. Additionally, Lyft Bikes has a simple interface where you can enter your current location and destination to see where the nearest bikes are and the exact bike route to take to reach your destination.

Lyft Bikes is also very convenient. Bikes are generally located in high traffic areas that are frequently visited. I am usually only a few minutes away from a bike. Similarly, when I get to my destination, there is usually a nearby bike drop-off location. I also like how I have the option to drop the bike off anywhere for a small additional fee.

For these three reasons, I believe this product stands out compared to its substitutes and alternatives.

Example #2: *What is your favorite product and why?*

My favorite product is TikTok, a short-form video sharing platform. There are three reasons why this product is my favorite: frictionless user experience, exceptional video discovery mechanism, and worldwide community.

TikTok is essentially television without a remote. As soon as you open the app, you are watching a short-form video. The only action you need to take is a single swipe to take you to the next video. There is no need to search for a video to watch or choose a video to watch. The app does it for you, removing the burden of choice and decision paralysis.

TikTok also has an exceptional video discovery mechanism driven by a tremendous amount of data. Every interaction is measured, such as likes, shares, comments, replays, and skips. Every aspect of the video is also captured, such as captions, sounds, hashtags, and effects. Even your device and account settings are taken into account, such as your language, country, and device type. Using all of this data, TikTok curates videos that you have a high probability of liking. The more you use the app, the better its video curation becomes.

Lastly, TikTok has a positive, worldwide community. Many videos on TikTok are not based on text or speaking. They are actions, such as dances, synced to music. This is universally understood, so you can understand videos from foreign creators that don't speak the same language as you.

What is your least favorite product and why?

This question is a variant of the "what is your favorite product?" question. Interviewers ask this question to try catch candidates off guard because nearly every candidate has a prepared answer to the "what is your favorite product?" question.

Features or characteristics that make a bad product are essentially the opposite of what makes a product great:

- **Poor usability**: The product has complicated user interfaces, confusing navigation, or inconsistent design patterns

- **Lack of reliability**: The product has unreliable performance, frequent crashes or errors, or downtime and service interruptions

- **Inadequate performance**: The product is slow, unresponsive, or resource-intensive without clear benefits

- **Limited functionality**: The product lacks essential features or does not meet user needs and expectations

- **Subpar quality**: The product has defective components or materials, is prone to wear and tear, has a short lifespan, or frequent breakdowns

- **Poor scalability**: The product is unable to handle increased loads or a larger user base

- **No customizability**: The product cannot be personalized to fit a user's specific needs or preferences

- **Outdated technology**: The product relies on obsolete and unsupported technologies or fails to adapt to industry standards

- **Limited integration**: The product cannot be used in conjunction with other products easily and seamlessly

- **Security concerns**: The product has vulnerabilities leading to data breaches, lack of proper encryption, lack of secure authentication, or insufficient protection against threats

- **No ethical considerations**: The product lacks transparency, has exploitative business practices, or disregards user privacy

- **Overly aggressive monetization**: The product has unfair pricing models or excessive ads and pop-ups

Similarly to how you would answer the "what's your favorite product?" question, you should also structure your answer. A structure will make your answer clearer and more concise for the interviewer to digest.

You can use the following simple, but effective structure:

- "[Product] is my least favorite product"

- "[1-2 sentence summary of what the product does]"
- "There are three reasons why this product is my least favorite: [reason 1], [reason 2], [reason 3]"
- "[Reason 1]…"
- "[Reason 2]…"
- "[Reason 3]…"
- "For these reasons, I believe this is a poor product that needs significant improvement"

As always, when giving the different reasons why you dislike the product, the most important thing is to make sure your reasons are specific.

Example: *What is your least favorite product and why?*

My least favorite product is Venmo. It is a digital wallet that lets you pay and request money from friends. There are three reasons why I dislike this product: it has many useless features, it is not as helpful as it could be, and the interface is not intuitive.

Venmo has a very useless main screen when you open the app. It shows a newsfeed of other people's transactions. I don't know who some of these people are and I also don't really care what transactions other people are making.

Venmo also has a "global" tab that shows transactions happening across the world. These are complete strangers and I don't ever foresee a use case for this feature.

Secondly, Venmo is not as helpful as it could be. When I create a new transaction, Venmo shows a list of friends that is sorted by the number of total transactions made. However, this sort does not take into account recency. For example, some friends have moved out and I'll likely never need to transact with them again. Still, these friends continue to show up at the top of every suggested list.

Lastly, Venmo's interface is not intuitive. For example, when I am trying to split $35 across 5 people, I can use the "÷" button to make the calculation. However, there is no "=" button to finish the calculation. You are supposed to click off the screen in order to finish the calculation, which is not intuitive.

Another example of poor user interface is that the request and pay buttons are both the same shade of blue. It takes me a few seconds every time to figure out which is the correct button I should tap. I've frequently tapped the wrong button before, requiring me to undo the transaction and make another one.

For these reasons, I believe that Venmo is a poor product that needs significant improvement.

How would you design or improve a particular product?

When asked how you would improve or design a product, resist the urge to list the first few ideas that come to your head. Instead, follow this systematic approach to demonstrate to the interviewer how you think about the product improvement and design process.

There are six main steps:

1. Define the goal

2. Identify a customer segment to target

3. Select a pain point to focus on

4. Brainstorm product improvements or designs

5. Assess which idea is best

6. Explain how you would test this

1. Define the goal

It is difficult to design or improve a product unless you have a specific and clear goal in mind. What are you trying to achieve?

The way you design or improve a product will change drastically depending on what you are trying to achieve. So, it is important that you confirm with the interviewer what the explicit goal is.

Are you trying to increase the number of monthly users? Are you trying to increase revenue per user? Is the goal to increase customer engagement? All of these different goals have drastically different solutions.

2. Identify a customer segment to target

The goal of this step is to focus and narrow down the scope of product improvement or design to one specific customer segment.

There are two reasons why you should do this.

One, customers can have a wide range of needs and preferences. Trying to improve or design a product that would benefit every single customer can be very challenging.

Two, by focusing on a specific customer segment, you can develop product improvements and designs that are more specific and tailored to the segment's needs. You will avoid suggesting product ideas that are generic and not impactful.

Therefore, start by listing the different customer segments that come to mind. Select one segment and provide a reason why you are focusing on that segment.

You might choose a segment because they are the largest segment or you might pick a segment if their needs are underserved.

3. Select a pain point to focus on

Brainstorm a list of pain points for the selected customer segment. These can be unmet customer needs or features of the product that customers find frustrating, time-consuming, or difficult to use.

Select one pain point and provide a reason why you are focusing on it. You might select a pain point if it is the most common, the most severe, or the most practical to solve for.

4. Brainstorm product improvements or designs

Now that you have chosen a pain point to focus on, brainstorm a list of different ways to solve for that pain point.

Try to have at least 3 - 5 different ideas. Include a few ideas that are creative and unconventional. This demonstrates originality and out-of-the-box thinking.

If you are having difficulty generating enough ideas, you can use the SCAMPER framework to help you brainstorm ideas.

SCAMPER stands for substitute, combine, adapt, modify, put to another use, eliminate, and reverse.

- **Substitute**: Replace an element or feature with something else

  Example: *Instead of using traditional fuel in cars, substituting it with a renewable energy source, such as electricity, led to the development of electric cars.*

- **Combine**: Merge different elements or features to create something new

  Example: *Combining a phone with a camera resulted in the creation of smartphones, which enables the user to both make calls and take pictures and videos on a single device.*

- **Adapt**: Alter an existing idea to better fit a new context or need

  Example: *The concept of car-sharing was adapted to bicycles, creating bike-sharing programs for urban commuting.*

- **Modify**: Make changes to the attributes, such as size, shape, color, or other characteristics

  Example: *Modify a traditional vending machine to make it sell freshly-cooked meals instead of packaged snacks and drinks.*

- **Put to another use**: Find new applications for an existing idea

  Example: *Virtual reality technology that was originally used for gaming can be put to another use for virtual travel experiences.*

- **Eliminate**: Remove unnecessary components or features

  Example: *The elimination of physical keyboards on smartphones led to the development of touchscreens.*

- **Reverse**: Change the order or perspective of elements or features

  Example: *Reverse the traditional classroom setting by implementing a "flipped classroom" approach, in which students learn new material at home through online resources and use class time for hands-on activities and discussion.*

5. Assess which idea is best

For this step, create a list of criteria to assess your different ideas. Common criteria include:

- Magnitude of impact
- User experience

- Cost
- Ease of implementation

Select the most important criteria based on the nature of the product and the pain point. Afterward, assess each of your product ideas based on the list of criteria you have developed.

You can assess your ideas either quantitatively or qualitatively.

The most common way to quantitatively score ideas is to give them one, two, or three points for each criteria. The idea that has the highest total number of points will be chosen.

Some criteria may be significantly more important than others. In this case, you can consider weighting the point values differently. For example, if the magnitude of impact is by far the most essential criteria, you can double the point value. Each idea will be given two, four, or six points for this criteria.

In assessing your ideas qualitatively, talk through how each idea performs on the criteria you have selected. Choose the improvement or design that has the most positive assessment overall.

6. Explain how you would test this

After you have selected your best idea, suggest how you would test whether this product improvement or design works. Specify what metrics you would want to measure to determine this.

This step is not always necessary, but it demonstrates to the interviewer that you can think like a product manager. Product roles involve a lot of testing and iterating on features and improvements.

A/B testing is the most common way to test a new product feature or design. In A/B testing, you compare the performance of two variations of a product against one another.

Typically, you would run an experiment in which one group of customers is given the original or older product and another group of customers is given the new and improved product.

After defining the right metrics to measure performance, you can determine which version of the product performs better.

Example #1: *How would you improve YouTube?*

For this question, I'll assume that the goal of the improvement is to increase user engagement on the platform, which can be measured as the amount of time a user spends on YouTube.

First, I'll think through the different customer segments and pick one to focus on. Three customer segments immediately come to mind:

- *Entertainment seekers are users that are bored who are looking for interesting videos to watch to pass the time*

- *Information seekers are users looking to learn a new skill or acquire information on a topic*

- *Music seekers are users looking for background music or sounds to play while they are doing something else*

Out of these segments, I will focus on entertainment seekers because this segment probably makes up the most significant portion of YouTube's user base.

Next, I'll identify a pain point to focus on. Entertainment seekers have a few different pain points:

- *The discovery process they go through to find entertaining videos takes time and effort*

- *Entertainment seekers find long videos dull and too slow to watch*

- *They get irritated when videos have clickbait titles that do not live up to expectations.*

Among these pain points, I'm going to focus on the tedious video discovery process because it is probably the biggest pain point for these users.

Now, I will brainstorm a few ideas on how to make the video discovery process easier.

- *YouTube could recommend videos based on videos that friends have seen. Since friends tend to have similar interests and tastes, these videos will likely be entertaining to entertainment seekers*

- *YouTube can have a continuous, curated video feed such that users do not have to search for the next video. Users can click on a skip button to immediately jump into the following video, which will be curated by an algorithm based on video history*

- *YouTube could send a curated playlist to the user each day. These videos would be selected by an algorithm based on video history*

I will assess each of these ideas on their impact, user experience, and ease of implementation.

The first idea, recommending videos based on videos that friends have seen, would have minimal impact if the user does not have friends that use YouTube frequently.

Additionally, this idea does not change the user experience much because entertainment seekers would still need to decide whether to watch a recommended video. The upside of this idea is that it would not be difficult to implement.

The second idea, having a continuous, curated video feed, could have a tremendous impact. It removes the burden of decision-making from entertainment seekers because YouTube videos are automatically played.

The user experience is also an improvement because the user only needs to click a skip button when they are bored. The downside of this idea is that developing a good algorithm could require substantial investment.

The third idea, sending a curated playlist to the user each day, would have some impact on users. The decision making process is slightly simplified because the user receives a shorter list of videos to choose from. However, once the playlist is finished, the user would still need to look for more videos on their own.

Additionally, the user experience is not ideal. Getting an email or notification every day can be annoying. The upside of this idea is that it is the most straightforward to implement.

Based on my assessment, the continuous, curated video feed seems to be the most promising.

To test this idea, I would develop a minimal viable product and use A/B testing to assess the performance of this feature.

One customer group would be given access to this feature while another customer group would not. I would measure the difference in minutes of video consumption between the two groups for one month to determine if user engagement has increased.

Example #2: *How would you improve Microsoft PowerPoint?*

For this question, I'll assume that the goal is to increase the number of monthly users of PowerPoint.

There is a wide variety of different customer segments that use PowerPoint. These include:

- *Students making presentations for their class assignments*
- *Working professionals making slides to present to their teams*
- *Sales people making pitch decks to sell a product or service*
- *Designers making mockups of webpages*
- *Game designers making simple interactive games*

For this question, I'm going to focus on the sales people that use PowerPoint to make pitch decks to sell a product or service because this is the segment I am most familiar with.

There are a few pain points that I can immediately think of for this customer segment:

- *Sales people find slide-making too time consuming*
- *Sales people don't know how to make their slides look good*
- *Sales people want to know they have created the best set of sales material to give themselves the highest chance of making the sale*

I have a few ideas that I think could tackle all of these pain points:

- *Add a slide design service to PowerPoint so that sales people can pay a professional to help them make their slides*
- *Create an online PowerPoint community that lets sales people share their best slides for others to use*
- *Provide a repository of slide templates designed by sales and PowerPoint professionals that have proven slide formats or structures that work*

I'm going to briefly run through the pros and cons of each of these options.

For the first product idea, the major hurdle I foresee is cost. Many sales people probably don't want to spend money every single time they need to make a pitch deck.

They could also alternatively find a design agency themselves to get their pitch deck made for them. Therefore, the only value this feature would add is removing the friction of researching and selecting a design agency to work with.

For the second product idea, I can think of several potential issues.

First, why would users want to share their best slides with others? Unless they are incentivized with money, the best sales people probably want to keep their secrets to themselves so that they remain a valuable asset to the company.

Additionally, sharing slides may pose a legal risk of accidentally sharing proprietary information.

Lastly, there would need to be a significant amount of effort involved in order to ensure that all of the slides shared are actually good slides. If sales people are uploading slides that they think are good, but are actually bad, then this will be of little value to others.

The third product idea seems to avoid a lot of the issues that the prior two ideas faced while addressing all three identified pain points.

This new feature would be free to use, which would encourage more sales people to use PowerPoint. It would still take sales people time to create their slides, but having a repository of templates would decrease the time they would spend because they are not starting from scratch.

This solution addresses the pain point of sales people not knowing how to make their slides look good.

Finally, this solution provides peace of mind that the slides being made are good because the slide templates are made by professionals.

To test this idea, I would develop a minimal viable product and use A/B testing to assess the performance of this feature. One customer group would be given access to this feature while another customer group would not.

I would measure whether customers use PowerPoint each month for a period of a year. I would hope that the group that has access to the feature will have higher retention, providing evidence that this feature would increase the number of monthly users.

Summary

- There are three common product questions:
    - What is your favorite product and why?
    - What is your least favorite product and why?
    - How would you design or improve a particular product?
- When picking a favorite product, make sure that it adheres to these five principles:
    - The product is one that you know well
    - The product is complex enough
    - The product is not ubiquitous
    - The product is not too obscure or niche
    - The product is relevant to the company
- You can use the following structure to answer the "what's your favorite product?" and "what's your least favorite product?" questions
    - "[Product] is my [favorite/least favorite] product"
    - "[1-2 sentence summary of what the product does]"
    - "There are three reasons why this product is my [favorite/least favorite]: [reason 1], [reason 2], [reason 3]"
    - "[Reason 1]…"
    - "[Reason 2]…"

  - "[Reason 3]…"
  - "For these reasons, I believe this is a [great/poor] product"

- There are six main steps in answering product improvement and design questions
  - Define the goal
  - Identify a customer segment to target
  - Select a pain point to focus on
  - Brainstorm product improvements or designs
  - Assess which idea is best
  - Explain how you would test this
- The SCAMPER framework can help you brainstorm new product ideas
  - Substitute
  - Combine
  - Adapt
  - Modify
  - Put to another use
  - Eliminate
  - Reverse

Practice

1. How would you improve the iPhone?

2. How would you design an alarm clock for the blind?

3. How would you improve LinkedIn's home page?

4. How would you improve Google Maps?

5. Design a reservation and payment system for a parking garage.

6. How would you improve Netflix?

7. What is your favorite product and why?

8. What is your least favorite product and why?

Solutions

1. How would you improve the iPhone?

   Let's assume that the goal is to improve customer satisfaction.

   First, let's identify the different customer segments and select one to focus on. There are a few different customer segments that come to mind:

   - *Entertainment users: This segment uses the iPhone for gaming, videos, and music*
   - *Photography users: This segment uses the iPhone for taking pictures and posting to social media*
   - *Productivity users: This segment uses the iPhone to handle emails, calendar events, and planning*

   I'd like to focus on photography users because almost everyone uses their iPhone's camera as their primary camera for day-to-day picture taking.

   There are many pain points with taking and managing photos on the iPhone:

   - *There is poor image quality if there is not enough light while taking a picture*
   - *It is difficult to clearly capture far away objects using the iPhone's camera*
   - *Selfies are annoying to take due to the location of the button that takes photos*
   - *Photos take up a lot of space, so not all of them can be kept on the iPhone*

- *It is time-consuming and tedious to manage all of the photos that are taken*

I'd like to focus on the last pain point because it is a pain point that I personally experience. After taking photos, it is time-consuming to look through all of the pictures to decide which ones to keep or delete.

Next, I'll brainstorm a few ways to address this pain point:

- *The iPhone could be configured to take multiple pictures over one to three seconds and save only the best image*

- *Photos are taken as usual, but the iPhone will make recommendations on what photos to delete when the user browses their photo album*

- *Photos are taken as usual, but there will be a feature added in which the iPhone highlights the best photos when the user browses their photo album*

I will assess each idea based on impact, user experience, and ease of implementation.

The first idea is very impactful since it automatically chooses and keeps the best photos. However, it can be a poor user experience because what the user sees on the camera may not be the photo that is taken.

Additionally, developing an algorithm that decides which photo is best will be difficult without large quantities of validated data.

The second idea is moderately impactful because it saves users some time. The user experience is excellent because the iPhone provides unprompted recommendations on photos to delete, but the user has ultimate decision rights.

Developing the algorithm for this feature will be easier than developing the algorithm for the first idea. It is easier to identify a bad photo than it is to identify a good photo. For poor photos, the algorithm could focus mainly on blurriness, closed eyes, and insufficient lighting.

The third idea is also moderately impactful in saving the user time. The user experience is great because it involves minimal effort from the user to see a curated collection of the best photos. However, developing an algorithm that selects good photos is likely difficult.

Therefore, I recommend that we improve the iPhone by adding a feature that suggests which pictures should be deleted.

We can test this feature through A/B testing. One group of users would have access to this feature while another group would not. We can measure differences in customer satisfaction related to photo management.

2. How would you design an alarm clock for the blind?

For this task, let's assume that the goal is to design an alarm clock that works reliably in waking up the user and is as easy to use as possible.

Additional alarm clock functionalities, such as checking the weather or listening to the radio, will not be considered.

The customer segment has already been defined, the blind.

There are four use cases that we need to design for:

- *Setting an alarm*
- *Checking to see if the alarm has been set*
- *Waking up the user*
- *Checking the time*

For each of these use cases, we can brainstorm a few potential ideas and evaluate the pros and cons for each to decide which design is optimal for our goals.

To set an alarm:

- *Design a voice assistant (e.g., similar to Siri or Alexa): This is quicker than a touchpad and can easily set an exact alarm time to the second. Additionally, the voice assistant can repeat the time set out loud so that the user knows the correct time has been set. However, there could be dictation issues for people with accents and this can only be done when the environment is relatively quiet.*

- *Design a braille touchpad: This would complicate the alarm clock by adding additional buttons. It would also take a longer time to set an alarm. The user would also need to take an additional step to check that the alarm has been set correctly once entered.*

To check if the alarm has been set:

- *Design a voice assistant that can answer the question of whether the alarm has been set: The user would not need to walk to the alarm clock to check if the alarm has been set. However, this needs to be done in a relatively quiet environment.*

- *Design a button that when pressed will play the time, the alarm set time, and whether the alarm is on/off: This provides all the information the user needs, but time-consuming as the user will need to hear all of the information each time. The user also needs to walk to the alarm clock to use this.*

- *Design a button that when pressed, vibrates if the alarm has been set: This communicates the information more quickly, but the user still needs to walk to the alarm clock to use this.*

To wake up the user:

- *Use visuals: If the user is blind, they likely won't be able to see anything, especially if they are asleep.*

- *Use sound: This is what almost all alarm clocks use.*

- *Use touch: The alarm clock can vibrate to wake the user. However, it is unclear if this would reliably wake up the user.*

- *Use smell or taste: This is a very unconventional approach to designing an alarm clock. Users probably don't want to be forced to smell or taste something. It is unclear whether the taste or smell would be strong enough to reliably wake up the user.*

To check the time:

- *Design mechanical braille buttons that change by the minute: This seems complicated to design and would likely increase the cost of the alarm clock.*

- *Design a button that says the time out loud when pressed: This is less complex than designing mechanical braille buttons that change by the minute. However, the user still needs to walk to the alarm clock to check the time.*

- *Design a voice assistant to say the time out loud when asked: The user would not need to walk to the alarm clock to check the time. However, this can only be done in a relatively quiet environment.*

Based on this, it seems that a voice assistant alarm clock that wakes up users with sound would be most suitable for our user.

3. How would you improve LinkedIn's home page?

There are a number of different potential goals that we could set:

- *Increase the number of monthly users*

- *Increase user time on the website*

- *Increase the number of actions per user*

- *Increase the number of ads displayed*

For this question, let's say that the goal is to increase the number of actions per user.

There are a number of different customer segments that use LinkedIn:

- *Working professionals looking for a job*
- *Recruiters looking to hire people*
- *Consulting firms doing industry research*
- *People looking to catch up on what colleagues are doing*

Let's focus on working professionals looking for a job. Their primary pain point is that they don't have a job or want a new job.

Therefore, they need a solution that makes it easy for them to find jobs that have openings, apply to jobs quickly and easily, prepare them for interviews, and help them manage all of their applications and upcoming interviews.

The main issue of LinkedIn's homepage is that it only shows a newsfeed of updates from people in the user's network and news articles. This is great for customers looking to catch up on what colleagues are doing, but is less useful for job seekers.

I think that the homepage can be improved by showing a different homepage to users that indicate that they are actively looking for a job.

There are a few important features that I think could be helpful to job seekers:

- *Display company postings for new jobs or roles to make it easier for users to find and apply to jobs*

- *Display a tracker of resumes submitted to make it easier for users to keep track of what they have applied to and the status of their application*

- *Display profiles of people that are in roles the user is interested in working in, making it easier for the user to network*

All three of these features could be put together into a new LinkedIn homepage for job seekers. The homepage would be divided into three sections: Job Openings, Application Status, and Networking Opportunities.

We can test this feature through A/B testing. One group of users would have access to this new homepage while another group would not. We can measure differences in:

- *Number of job postings viewed*

- *Number of job postings applied to*

- *Number of application statuses checked*

- *Number of profiles viewed*

- *Number of messages sent*

4. How would you improve Google Maps?

   There are a number of different potential goals that we could set:

   - *Increase the number of monthly users*

   - *Increase the number of new users*

   - *Increase the time spent on the app*

   - *Increase the number of ads shown*

For this question, let's say that the goal is to increase the number of users per month.

There are a number of different customer segments that use Google Maps:

- *People trying to get from point A to point B*
- *People looking for fun things to do nearby*
- *People trying to list their business on Google Maps*
- *People looking for hiking trails*
- *People planning vacations*

Let's focus on people that are looking for fun things to do nearby since this is a segment I find myself belonging to. There are a few pain points that these users face:

- *They don't know what fun things to do are nearby and what to pick*
- *They don't know what is open*
- *They don't know if they need to make a reservation*

Let's focus on the pain point of searching and picking a fun thing to do nearby. There a few potential solutions I can think of:

- *Add search options to look for fun (e.g., outdoor activities, indoor activities)*
- *Show ads in the app of fun businesses (e.g., mini-golf, arcades, rock climbing)*
- *Add a feature where users can swipe through different fun businesses nearby*

- *Add a feature similar to Google's former "I'm feeling lucky" button that takes the user to the first search result for "fun"*

The first idea can work quite well. Google Maps already has search options for places such as "restaurants" or "gas stations," so expanding this to include fun activities could be viable.

The second idea would generate more revenue for Google, but that is not the goal we are aiming for. Instead, showing too many ads could upset customers, which could actually decrease the number of monthly users if users feel ad fatigue.

The third idea makes it easy to look through different options for fun. However, the swiping mechanism does not really fit Google's brand. It would also take a lot of swipes for someone to see all the potential options for fun.

The fourth idea makes it easy for users to find something, but is unlikely to resonate with users due to their wide range of interests.

Therefore, I believe the first idea seems best. It also is aligned with Google's company goal of giving users the power to search for information.

We can test this feature through A/B testing. One group of users would have access to this new feature while another group would not. We can measure differences in number of monthly users over a one year period.

5. Design a reservation and payment system for a parking garage.

   Let's assume the goal for this question is to increase the number of monthly users in a parking garage.

   There are several different customer segments we could focus on:

   - *Customers that want a quick and convenient parking experience*

- *Customers that want parking spots that are close to their destination of interest*
- *Customers that want the most affordable prices for parking*
- *Customers that want to know that their parked car will be safe from thieves and break-ins*
- *Customers that park their car frequently and want to ensure that there will always be a spot for their car*

Let's focus on the first customer segment, customers that want a quick and convenient parking experience, since that is probably the largest customer segment.

To design the best reservation and payment system for a parking garage, let's first think through what the typical parking garage experience looks like.

- *Customer enters the garage by pushing a button on a machine to open the parking garage gate and receive a ticket*
- *Customer drives through the garage, looking for an empty spot*
- *Customer has to wait for cars to park that are ahead of them*
- *Customer parks their car*
- *When leaving, the customer has to find their ticket and pay for parking at a machine*
- *Customer leaves the garage by submitting a paid ticket on their way out*

Now, let's re-imagine the parking experience if we redesigned it to make it as quick and convenient as we can:

- *Customer drives right into the garage, not needing to stop to receive a ticket or wait for a gate to open. This can be accomplished by:*
    - *Capturing the car's license plate*
    - *Having a unique RFID tag in each car that is read*
    - *Requiring users to pre-pay for parking in advance*
- *Customer drives through the garage directly to their designated parking spot, not needing to wait for any other cars ahead of them or search for an open space. This can be accomplished by:*
    - *Having sensors at each parking spot to detect if the spot is free and assigning cars to the furthest parking spot to avoid lines forming*
    - *Requiring users to provide their estimated arrival time in advance and using an algorithm to determine how to assign parking spots to minimize traffic*
    - *Having parking valet park each car for the customer*
- *When leaving, the customer can drive through the exit, not needing to submit a ticket or wait for a gate to open. This can be accomplished by:*
    - *Automatically mailing a bill to the address associated with the car's license plate*
    - *Automatically billing a card on file that was registered with the RFID tag*
    - *Not requiring payment at time of exit because users were required to pre-pay in advance*

We can assess each idea based on their impact, ease of implementation, and cost. After doing this, our reservation and payment system for a parking garage may look like the following:

- *Car enters the garage; license plate is captured by a camera along with the entry time*
- *Sensors at each parking spot determine if the spot is occupied or free*
- *Upon entry, a parking spot is assigned to the car and displayed upon entry for the driver to see*
    - *If it is a low traffic time (can be determined by dynamically tracking how many cars are in the garage), the nearest parking spot will be assigned*
    - *If it is a high traffic time, the furthest parking spot will be assigned to minimize traffic inside the garage*
- *Driver drives to the assigned spot and parks the car*
- *To leave, the car exits the garage; license plate is captured by a camera along with the exit time*
    - *If it is the first time that car has parked in the garage, a bill will be mailed to the address associated with the license plate; the driver has the option to add a credit card or bank account to the parking account associated with their license plate number*
    - *If the car has parked in the garage before, the user's credit card or bank account is automatically charged*

6. How would you improve Netflix?

Let's assume the goal for this question is to increase customer retention.

There are several different customer segments we could target:

- *Families: Viewers that use Netflix for its extensive library of family-friendly content*
- *Binge-watchers: Users who prefer watching entire seasons or multiple episodes in one sitting*
- *Movie buffs: Movie enthusiasts who have a specific interest in films, including classic movies and independent films*
- *Language learners: Viewers who leverage foreign language content and subtitles to enhance language skills*
- *Busy professionals: Individuals who don't have much free time, but still want to watch entertaining content*

Let's focus on the busy professionals segment since that is a segment that is most likely to cancel their Netflix subscription.

There are several pain points that busy professionals experience when using Netflix:

- *Decision fatigue in selecting what content to watch*
- *Difficulty keeping up with the latest releases due to demanding work schedules*
- *Interrupted viewing experience due to work-related calls, emails, or other responsibilities that leads to a fragmented and less enjoyable viewing experience*
- *Desire for more short-form content that can be fit into shorter breaks*

- *Experiencing guilt or concerns about spending too much time on entertainment platforms such as Netflix, especially if they perceive it as impacting their overall productivity*

Let's focus on the pain point of keeping up with the latest releases due to demanding work schedules. Since working professionals don't have much free time, they aren't able to stay up to date on the latest episodes that get released.

Let's brainstorm some solutions to this pain point:

- *Weekly recap emails: Introduce a weekly email digest summarizing what happened in the latest movie or episode releases*

- *Abridged versions of episodes: Cut out unnecessary scenes from movies and episodes to shorten the length of watch time needed*

- *Increase playback speed: Add a feature to allow users to watch a movie or episode at 3x or higher playback speed*

- *Provide a curated shortlist of what to watch: Recommend a subset of new movie and episode releases to users based on what is most trending or the most highly reviewed*

Let's briefly assess each idea.

The first idea is likely not going to help retain users. People subscribe to Netflix to watch movies and episodes, not to read text summaries. Netflix users can also find summaries of episodes online for free, so this idea would not add much value.

The second idea is interesting. It reduces the amount of time a user needs to spend watching a movie or episode in order to know what is going on. Abridged versions of episodes make it easier for working professionals to fit Netflix into their schedule. This would also help working professionals feel productive since they are consuming the same amount of content that others are watching, but in a shorter period of time.

The major downside is that abridged episodes may not be as entertaining or comprehensive as watching the full episode. It would also take extra work to create an abridged version of every new release.

The third idea is very feasible to implement, but not practical. Most users of Netflix can probably only watch at 1.5x speed at most without having an impact on comprehension. Watching at higher speeds likely also negatively impacts the viewing experience.

The fourth idea is also very feasible to implement. However, it doesn't necessarily solve the pain point we are focusing on. Busy professionals are likely already prioritizing what new movies and episodes to watch. So, providing a curated shortlist does not really address their pain point of not having enough time to watch the things that they care about.

Based on this brief assessment, we can propose testing the second idea of creating abridged versions of movies and episodes.

We can launch this feature to a subset of users that are busy professionals and measure customer retention changes compared to our control group of users that do not have this feature.

7. Marketing Questions

What are marketing questions?

Marketing questions ask you to develop a plan or strategy to market and sell a particular product.

Examples of marketing questions include:

- What customer segments would you target?
- How would you market or sell this product to customers?
- How would you price this product?

The first question asks you to identify and define the specific groups of customers who would benefit most from the product.

The second question asks you to outline a comprehensive marketing plan that may include targeting, messaging, and marketing channels.

Finally, the third question evaluates your understanding of pricing strategies. It requires you to consider factors such as production costs, competition, and value perception.

What are interviewers looking for?

Interviewers are looking for three major skills and qualities when asking marketing questions:

- **Customer-centric approach**: Interviewers are interested in whether you can put yourself in the shoes of the customer to understand their needs, pain points, and preferences

- **Creativity and innovation**: Interviewers are interested in your ability to come up with creative marketing campaigns and initiatives that will set the product apart from the competition

- **Analytic thinking**: Interviewers want to see that you can make data-driven decisions when determining the optimal price for a product

How to answer marketing questions?

For marketing questions, resist the urge to list the first few ideas that come to your head.

Instead, follow a systematic approach to demonstrate to the interviewer that you can think about product marketing in a strategic and structured way.

There are two frameworks you can use to help you answer these questions:

1. STP framework

2. 4 P's framework

STP stands for segmentation, targeting, and positioning. To develop a marketing strategy, use this framework to identify a customer segment and positioning statement for your product.

Segmentation

The first step is to understand how the market is segmented. Customers have a wide variety of needs and preferences. Therefore, a broad marketing strategy targeting every customer will not be as effective as a tailored marketing strategy focused on a specific customer segment.

You will need to decide what type of segmentation makes the most sense for your product. You can segment customers on needs, use cases, or various demographics, such as age, geography, income, lifestyle, and attitudes.

Example: *If you are marketing a social media platform, it may make sense to segment customers by age. If you are selling a laptop, it may make sense to segment customers by use case. If you are selling enterprise software, you might segment by company size.*

At the end of this step, you should have a list of the different customer segments.

Targeting

The next step is to evaluate the attractiveness of each segment and choose a target segment to focus on. There are many different factors to consider when selecting a target segment:

- Which segment is the largest?
- Which segment is growing the quickest?
- What segment is the most profitable?
- Which segment is the most accessible?
- Which segment is the best fit for your product?

- Which segment has the potential for the most improvement?
- Which segment is the most influenced by marketing?

Once you have selected a customer segment to focus on, you can move onto the next step, developing a positioning statement.

Positioning

Now, you will determine how to position and communicate the product to potential customers.

Your positioning and communication of the product should be tailored to the specific needs and preferences of the customer segment you have decided to focus on. In determining how to position the product, ask yourself the following questions:

- What makes this customer segment different from others?
- What does this customer segment value?
- What are the attitudes or beliefs of this customer segment?

Below are a few examples of positioning statements from well-known companies:

- **Amazon**: For customers who want to purchase a wide variety of products online, Amazon offers a one-stop shopping experience
- **Apple**: For technology users who want a seamless experience, Apple leads the industry with the most innovative and easy-to-use products
- **Disney**: For consumers looking for unique entertainment, Disney provides magical memories and experiences

Having a positioning statement will help you decide the best way to market the product. To do that, you will move onto the next framework, the 4 P's.

The 4 P's stands for product, place, promotion, and price. The goal of 4 P's is to define the best way to market the product.

Product

If there are multiple products or different versions of a product, you will need to decide which product to market. To do this, you will need to fully understand the benefits and points of differentiation of each product.

Select the product that best fits customer needs and the positioning statement you developed for the segment you are focusing on.

Place

You will need to decide where the product will be sold to customers. Different customer segments have different purchasing habits and behaviors. Therefore, some distribution channels will be more effective than others.

Should the product be sold directly to the customer online? Should the product be sold in the company's stores? Should the product be sold through retail partners instead?

Promotion

You will need to decide how to spread information about the product to customers. Different customer segments have different media consumption habits and preferences. Therefore, some promotional strategies will be more effective than others.

Promotional techniques and strategies include advertising, social media marketing, email marketing, search engine marketing, video marketing, and public relations. Select the strategies and techniques that will be the most effective.

Price

You will need to decide how to price the product. Pricing is important because it determines the profits and the quantity of units sold. Pricing can also communicate information on the quality or value of the product.

If you price the product too high, you may be pricing the product above your customer segment's willingness to pay. This leads to lost sales.

If you price the product too low, you may be losing potential profit from customers who were willing to pay a higher price. You may also be losing profits from customers who perceive the product as low-quality due to a low price point.

There are three pricing strategies you should be familiar with:

Pricing based on costs: Set a price to achieve a certain amount of profit or profit margin. It usually does not make sense to price a product below the total costs to produce that product. Pricing based on costs helps you determine the minimum price you should set the product at.

Example: *Your company produces custom-made dining tables. The total cost of producing a dining table, including materials, labor, and overhead, is $400. You would like a reasonable profit margin of 20%. Therefore, you decide to price the product at $500.*

Pricing based on value provided: This strategy determines price by quantifying the benefits that the product provides customers. You can only charge as much as the perceived value you provide customers. This pricing strategy helps you determine the maximum price you can set.

Example: *You are launching a new software application that streamlines project management for businesses. After conducting customer interviews, you discover that your software significantly increases team productivity, leading to an estimated annual cost savings of $50,000. You decide to set a price of $20,000 per year to capture a fraction of the value that your product provides customers.*

Pricing based on competition: Set a price based on what competitors are charging for products similar to yours. This pricing strategy helps you determine where in between the minimum price and maximum price the optimal price point falls.

***Example**: Your company sells jeans. After researching the prices of similar jeans at nearby stores, you notice that a popular style of jeans is priced at an average of $80 by your competitors. To remain competitive and attract price-sensitive customers, you decide to price your jeans at $70.*

Most of the time, you'll need to use a combination of all three pricing strategies to determine the optimal price point.

Marketing question examples

***Example #1**: You sell household cleaning products. What customer segments can you think of and how would you target them?*

There are eight different customer segments that I can immediately think of:

- *Environmentally conscious consumers: People who prioritize eco-friendly and sustainable products to minimize their environmental impact.*

  → We can target this segment by emphasizing the product's eco-friendly certifications, natural ingredients, and biodegradable packaging.

- *Busy professionals and families: People with busy schedules who seek efficient and convenient cleaning solutions*

  → We can target this segment by highlighting time-saving features, such as quick-drying formulas, easy application methods, and multi-purpose products

- *Allergy and sensitivity sufferers: People who have allergies or sensitivities to common cleaning chemicals and seek hypoallergenic and non-toxic alternatives*

  → We can target this segment by promoting the product as hypoallergenic, fragrance-free, and free from harsh chemicals. We

can provide endorsements or recommendations from dermatologists or allergists to build trust.

- *Pet owners: People who have pets and need cleaning products that effectively tackle pet-related messes and odors*

  → We can target this segment by showcasing the product's ability to remove pet stains, hair, and odors. We can provide testimonials from satisfied pet owners.

- *Health and safety-conscious consumers: People who prioritize cleanliness and hygiene for their well-being, especially in light of health concerns*

  → We can target this segment by highlighting the product's effectiveness in killing germs, bacteria, and viruses. We can mention any relevant certifications or endorsements from health organizations or testing results from scientists.

- *Minimalists: People who prefer streamlined and versatile cleaning solutions to reduce clutter and simplify their cleaning routines*

  → We can target this segment by showcasing the product's versatility for multiple surfaces or purposes. We can also emphasize the product's compact packaging and space-saving design.

- *Budget-conscious consumers: People who prioritize affordability and seek cost-effective cleaning solutions*

  → We can target this segment by offering competitive pricing, bundle deals, and promotions to showcase the product's value for money. We can highlight the product's effectiveness in relation to its affordability.

- *Luxury homeowners: Wealthy individuals who value premium quality and are willing to invest in luxurious, high-end cleaning products*

  → We can target this segment by positioning the product as a premium product with high-quality ingredients, elegant packaging,

and exclusive scents. We can collaborate with luxury retailers or spa resorts for distribution.

Example #2: *How would you sell the Microsoft Surface tablet to an 80-year-old senior citizen?*

First, I'll identify the distinguishing attributes of this segment to develop a positioning statement for the product. Some characteristics of senior citizens are that they:

- *Value keeping in touch with family*
- *Have a lot of free time because they are retired*
- *Watch television and read newspapers*
- *Find technology challenging to use*

From this, I propose the following positioning statement:

For senior citizens looking to connect and stay close to family members, the Microsoft Surface tablet is an easy way to bring families together

Senior citizens do not have a tremendous amount of money to spend, so it probably makes sense to sell them a basic version of the Microsoft Surface tablet. They do not need additional storage or high-performance upgrades.

Moving onto the marketing strategy, Microsoft should advertise on television, running ads that show senior citizens using the tablet to video chat with their grandchildren. Microsoft should run these ads during the late afternoon or early evening, when most senior citizens watch television.

For distribution, senior citizens typically do not make purchases online. It can also be difficult for them to go to retail stores because of their age and limited transportation options.

Therefore, the ads should provide a phone number for senior citizens to call to make their purchases. The product will be delivered directly to their front doorsteps to reduce any friction in purchasing.

For pricing, Microsoft should advertise the lower price of a basic tablet model to increase the likelihood that senior citizens will make a purchase.

At a high-level, this is the marketing strategy I would use to sell the Microsoft Surface tablet to an 80-year-old citizen.

Example #3: *How would you price a smartphone case that is made of high-quality, durable materials and has additional features, including a built-in card holder and a kickstand?*

There are three strategies we can use to price this product:

- *Cost-based pricing*
- *Value-based pricing*
- *Competition-based pricing*

Let's consider each of these.

Cost based pricing:

We can calculate the total cost of producing the item. This includes the cost of raw materials, labor, packaging, and overhead. We can then add a desired profit margin.

Value-based pricing:

We can identify the specific benefits and value propositions of our smartphone case. The built-in card holder and kickstand make the smartphone case both more convenient and versatile for users. We can then estimate how much customers would be willing to pay for these added benefits. This can be done through market research or surveys to understand customer perceptions of value. We would then set a price that reflects the perceived value provided by the product.

Competition-based pricing:

We can research the prices of similar smartphone cases in the market. Specifically, we can look into competitors that have cases with similar features and build quality. If our product offers any unique features or advantages, we may be able to price our product higher. Else, we would likely need to price the product comparably to our competitors.

Summary

- For marketing questions that ask you to develop a marketing plan or strategy, use the STP and 4 P's framework
- The STP framework helps identify a customer segment and positioning statement for your product
    - **Segmentation**: Create a list of customer segments
    - **Targeting**: Select one segment to focus on
    - **Positioning**: Decide how to position and communicate the product
- The 4 P's framework helps define the best way to market a product
    - **Product**: Decide which product or version of the product to market
    - **Place**: Decide where the product will be sold
    - **Promotion**: Decide how to spread information about the product to customers
    - **Price**: Decide how to price the product

Practice

1. How would you market Instagram to small- and medium-sized businesses?

2. How would you price a premium smart thermostat with advanced energy-saving features?

3. You sell noise-canceling headphones with advanced AI-driven features. What customer segments can you think of and how would you target them?

4. You are the product manager for a language learning app targeting high school students. How would you market the app to educators and school administrators to encourage its adoption in the classroom?

5. How would you price a subscription-based productivity software aimed at professionals and businesses?

6. Imagine you are the product manager for a fitness tracking app that provides personalized workout recommendations and real-time feedback. Identify potential customer segments for this app and determine a targeting strategy for each segment.

Solutions

1. How would you market Instagram to small- and medium-sized businesses?

   I'll first identify the characteristics of this customer segment. These businesses typically:

   - *Don't have much money to spend on marketing*
   - *Don't have a full-time employee for social media*
   - *Value having a personal touch with customers*
   - *Have difficulty competing against larger businesses*

   Based on these characteristics, one potential positioning statement is the following:

   For businesses that want to stay in touch with customers, but have a limited budget, Instagram is a powerful, low-maintenance platform to develop meaningful relationships with customers.

   Moving onto marketing strategy, we want to market a business Instagram account.

   We should price the product as free because small- and medium-sized businesses have limited budgets. We may even want to offer them free credit for Instagram advertising.

   Once these businesses have used the platform and see Instagram's value, they can be convinced to spend money on Instagram's premium offerings.

   We do not want larger businesses to take advantage of these free offerings because they have money to spend.

   Therefore, digital marketing is likely the most effective channel. Through online ads, we can specifically target small- and medium-sized businesses and avoid targeting larger companies.

2. How would you price a premium smart thermostat with advanced energy-saving features?

   There are three strategies we can use to price this product:

   - *Cost-based pricing*
   - *Value-based pricing*
   - *Competition-based pricing*

   Let's consider each of these.

   Cost-based pricing: Calculate the total cost of producing the smart thermostat. This includes the cost of materials, manufacturing, labor, and overhead. Then, add a desired profit margin.

   Value-based pricing: Identify the specific benefits of the smart thermostat. This could include energy savings, convenience, compatibility with smart home systems, and potential rebates or incentives. Estimate how much customers would be willing to pay for these added benefits and set a price that reflects the perceived value provided by the smart thermostat.

   Competition-based pricing: Research the prices of similar smart thermostats in the market. If the product offers more advanced technology or benefits, you could justify a higher price. If it's on par with competitors, you should aim for a similar price point.

3. You sell noise-canceling headphones with advanced AI-driven features. What customer segments can you think of and how would you target them?

   There are four different customer segments that come to mind:

   - *Frequent travelers: Individuals that want peace and quiet during their journeys. They often face noisy environments in airports, planes, and public transportation*

→ Emphasize the superior noise cancellation technology for a tranquil travel experience. Highlight the long battery life to cater to extended flights. Showcase the headphones' compact and foldable design for easy portability

- *Working professionals: Individuals that need headphones that can enhance their productivity, whether it's for important calls or focused work in noisy office environments.*

  → Highlight high-quality audio for clear calls, comfortable fit for all-day wear, advanced noise isolation for a distraction-free work environment, and seamless integration for virtual meetings

- *Gaming enthusiasts: Individuals that require headphones that will deliver immersive sound quality to enhance their gaming experience*

  → Emphasize spatial audio for a 360-degree gaming experience. Highlight low-latency audio transmission for competitive gaming. Mention a comfortable design for long gaming sessions.

- *Audiophiles: Individuals that are passionate about high-fidelity audio quality and appreciate headphones that offer a personalized, premium listening experience.*

  → Highlight high-fidelity audio quality and premium materials, customizable sound profiles for individual preferences, and comfortable fit for long listening sessions.

4. You are the product manager for a language learning app targeting high school students. How would you market the app to educators and school administrators to encourage its adoption in the classroom?

   I'll first identify the characteristics and pain points of this customer segment. Educators and school administrators typically:

- *Have limited resources for educational materials, technology, and professional development due to budget constraints*
- *Have overloaded schedules with responsibilities ranging from teaching and administrative tasks to meetings and professional development*
- *Have difficulty keeping students engaged and motivated in the learning process*
- *Need to ensure that teaching methods and materials align with curriculum standards and educational objectives*
- *Need to address the diverse learning needs and abilities of students, making it challenging to cater to everyone effectively*

Based on these characteristics, one potential positioning statement is the following:

For educators that want the best learning experience for their students, but have limited time and budget, this language learning app provides engaging and curriculum-aligned learning that is personalized to the needs of each student.

Moving onto marketing strategy, here's how we would best target educators and school administrators:

- *Market the product at educator conferences and teacher development trainings*
- *We should try to partner with educational associations to gain endorsements and promote the app as a recommended language learning tool within the educational community*
- *The app should be priced on a per student basis since schools can vary greatly in size.*

- *The app should be priced such that it is a cost-effective solution for schools (e.g., saving them the costs of hiring teachers, buying textbooks, paying for teacher training); consider offering a discount for schools*

5. How would you price a subscription-based productivity software aimed at professionals and businesses?

   There are three strategies we can consider to price this product:

   - *Cost-based pricing*
   - *Value-based pricing*
   - *Competition-based pricing*

   Let's consider each of these.

   Cost-based pricing: Begin by calculating the total cost associated with developing, maintaining, and supporting the productivity software. This includes development costs, ongoing maintenance, server expenses, and customer support.

   Then, add a desired profit margin to cover these costs and generate a desired level of profit.

   Value-based pricing: Identify and quantify the specific benefits that the productivity software offers to professionals and businesses. This could include increased efficiency, collaboration features, integration with other tools, and enhanced project management capabilities.

   Afterwards, estimate how much customers would be willing to pay for these added benefits. Consider conducting market research, surveys, or interviews to understand the perceived value of the software. Set a price that aligns with the perceived value and the positive impact the software brings to users.

   Competition-based pricing: Research the prices of similar productivity software in the market targeting the same professional and business segments. Understand the pricing models, feature offerings, and positioning of competitors.

If the software offers unique features or an advanced set of capabilities compared to competitors, consider pricing the software at a premium. If it competes directly on features and functionalities, aim for a competitive price point.

6. Imagine you are the product manager for a fitness tracking app that provides personalized workout recommendations and real-time feedback. Identify potential customer segments for this app and determine a targeting strategy for each segment.

   There are a few different customer segments we could target:

   - *Fitness beginners: Individuals who are new to exercising and looking for guidance and support*

     → Emphasize the app's user-friendly interface and beginner-friendly workout plans

   - *Busy professionals: Working individuals with limited time for exercise*

     → Highlight the app's quick workout options, time-efficient training plans, and the ability to seamlessly integrate with busy schedules

   - *Health-conscious individuals: People who prioritize overall health and wellness*

     → Showcase the app's holistic approach to health, including features for nutrition tracking, sleep monitoring, and stress management

   - *Technology enthusiasts: Individuals who are early adopters of technology and enjoy incorporating it into their daily lives*

→ *Highlight the app's cutting-edge technology and unique tech-driven features*

- *Competitive athletes: Individuals engaged in competitive sports or serious athletic training*

  → *Showcase the app's advanced analytics, performance tracking, and personalized training plans tailored for competitive athletes*

- *Social fitness groups: Individuals who prefer working out in social settings or groups*

  → *Highlight the app's social features, such as group challenges, leaderboards, and the ability to connect with friends for shared workouts*

- *Seniors: Older individuals interested in maintaining or improving their fitness levels*

  → *Emphasize the app's adaptability for various fitness levels, easy-to-follow instructions, and features tailored to the specific needs and preferences of seniors (e.g., larger text font size, louder notification sounds)*

8. Estimation Questions

What are estimation questions?

Estimation questions ask you to estimate a particular number or figure by making assumptions and performing calculations.

Examples of estimation questions include:

- Estimate the number of people who use social media platforms globally
- Estimate the number of daily taxi rides in New York City
- How many Amazon packages are stolen in the United States each year?

One of the most common types of estimation questions are market sizing questions, which ask you to estimate the annual spending of a specific category of product.

This involves determining the total addressable market (TAM), which represents the maximum revenue a product could generate if it captured 100% of the market.

Examples of market sizing questions include:

- How many iPhones are sold in the United States each year?
- What is the market size of electric cars globally?
- How many burgers does McDonalds sell each year?

These questions may seem tough to answer, but with practice, estimation questions become straight forward and repetitive.

What are interviewers looking for?

For estimation questions, you are not assessed on how close your estimate is to the actual number. It is great if your estimate is close to the actual number, but what is more important is demonstrating how you get to your estimate.

Estimation questions assess a variety of skills, including:

- **Problem solving skills**: Developing a structured approach to come up with an estimate
- **Quantitative skills**: Making numerical calculations quickly and accurately
- **Creativity and innovation**: Using creative methods to approach the problem if there is a lack of data
- **Adaptability**: Adjusting your approach or assumptions based on the interviewer's feedback
- **Communication skills**: Articulating the steps taken to arrive at an estimate to ensure that the interviewer can follow your thought process

How do you answer estimation questions?

There are two different methods to tackle estimation questions. You can either take a top-down approach or a bottom-up approach.

Top-down approach

In a top-down approach, start with a large number and then refine and break down the number until you get your answer.

Example: *How many iPhones does Apple sell in the U.S. each year?*

Using a top-down strategy, you could develop the following approach to answer this question:

- *Start with the number of people in the U.S.*
- *Estimate the percentage of people that have cell phones*
- *Estimate the percentage of cell phones that are iPhones*
- *Estimate the frequency in which a person purchases a new iPhone each year*
- *Multiply these numbers to determine the number of iPhones sold each year*

Following this approach, we'll assume a U.S. population size of 320 million people. If 75% of people have cell phones and 30% of cell phones are iPhones, this gives us 72 million iPhones.

If a person purchases a new iPhone every two years, that means 36 million iPhones are sold in the U.S. each year.

Bottom-up approach

In a bottom-up approach, start with a small number and then build up and increase the number until you get your answer.

***Example**: How many iPhones does Apple sell in the U.S. each year?*

Using a bottom-up strategy, you could develop the following approach:

- *Start with a single Apple store*
- *Estimate the number of visits per day*
- *Calculate the number of visits per year*
- *Estimate the percentage of visits that lead to purchases*
- *Estimate the percentage of purchases that include the iPhone*
- *Multiply by the number of Apple stores in the U.S. to get the total number of iPhones sold in Apple stores*
- *Estimate the percentage of iPhone sales made through non-Apple stores to determine the number of iPhones sold across all stores*
- *Estimate the percentage of iPhone sales that are made online to determine the total number of iPhones sold in the U.S.*

Following this approach, let's assume a single Apple store gets 1,000 visits per day. If the store is open 360 days per year, an Apple store gets 360,000 visits per year.

If 25% of visits lead to purchases and 60% of purchases include an iPhone, one Apple store sells 54,000 iPhones per year.

If there are 300 Apple stores in the U.S., then 16.2 million iPhones are sold in Apple stores each year.

If non-Apple stores account for 25% of total iPhone store sales, then 21.6 million iPhones are sold in physical stores each year.

If online iPhone sales account for 40% of total iPhone purchases, then 36 million iPhones are sold in the U.S.

As you can see, both the top-down and bottom-up strategy can lead you to the same answer.

When answering estimation questions, choose the approach that is easier for you. Most people find the top-down strategy to be simpler.

How do you make reasonable assumptions?

One of the most difficult parts of solving estimation questions is making reasonable assumptions.

There are three major strategies to make reasonable assumptions:

1. Use personal experiences

Drawing from personal experiences provides a good starting point for making reasonable assumptions.

What you experience and go through in life is likely not too different from what others go through for most situations.

Example: *You need to make an assumption for how many cups of coffee the average coffee-drinker consumes. You have a few data points in your life that you can leverage:*

- *You drink 2 cups per day*
- *Your mom drinks 2 cups per day*
- *Your dad drinks 3 cups per day*
- *Your best friend drinks 1 cup per day*

The average of these data points is 2 cups per day. Therefore, you can assume that people drink an average of 2 cups per day.

2. Use a proxy

If you are finding it difficult to make an assumption for a specific number or metric, it may be easier to make an assumption for a different but related number or metric and make adjustments to it.

Example: *You are trying to make an assumption for the number of people that live in Canada.*

You know that Canada has a smaller population than the United States, which has a population of over 300 million. You take a guess that Canada has 15% of the population of the United States.

Therefore, you estimate that the population of Canada is roughly 45 million.

3. Use lower and upper bounds

If you are finding it difficult to even get started making a particular assumption, it may be helpful to first identify the lower and upper bounds.

Once you have a sense of the lower and upper bounds of an estimate, you can make an assumption that falls somewhere in-between these limits.

It is often easier to pick a number when given a range than to just pick a number without any further context.

Example: *You are trying to estimate the number of people that attend a college basketball game.*

You know that a college basketball gym sits more people than a high school basketball gym, but sits fewer people than an NFL stadium.

You know that high school basketball gyms can seat 100-300 people.

You know that NFL stadiums can seat 60,000-80,000 people.

These are your lower and upper bounds.

Looking at this range, you believe that the size of a college basketball gym is closer to the lower bound than the upper bound. Therefore, you estimate that a college basketball game has 10,000 attendees.

Estimation math tips

It can be challenging to make accurate math calculations when you are under the immense pressure of an interview.

Follow the math tips below to help simplify your math calculations and greatly decrease the chances that you make a mistake.

1. Work with units instead of numbers

This math tip will help prevent you from having too many zeroes or too few zeroes in your final answer. This is by far the most common math mistake that candidates make.

The key to never making this type of mistake is to work with units instead of numbers.

What do we mean by this?

We can simplify how we write thousands, millions, and billions by using the letters "K," "M," and "B."

For example, we can re-write 17,000 as 17K, 140,000,000 as 140M, and 8,100,000,000 as 8.1B.

When doing math, all we need to do is to multiply or divide the numbers, multiply or divide the letters, and then put the two together to get our answer.

The only thing you need to remember is that:

- K * K = M
- M * K = B

- M / K = K
- B / M = K
- B / K = M

***Example #1**: What is 12,000 * 18,000?*

*We can re-write this as 12K * 18K.*

*12 * 18 = 216.*

*K * K = M.*

Therefore, putting these two calculations together, our final answer is 216M or 216,000,000.

***Example #2**: What is 1,680,000,000 divided by 120,000.*

1,680,000,000 can be re-written as 1,680M.

120,000 can be re-written as 120K.

1,680 / 120 = 14.

M / K = K.

Therefore, putting these two calculations together, our final answer is 14K or 14,000.

2. Use the distributive property

The distributive property can be used to make multiplication much easier.

Instead of directly multiplying two numbers, you can express one of the numbers as the sum of two numbers. You can then multiply each of these two numbers by the other number and add them up to get the final answer.

Example*: What is 303 * 60?*

*We can re-write this as (300 + 3) * 60.*

*300 * 60 = 18,000.*

*3 * 60 = 180.*

Adding 18,000 and 180, we get our final answer of 18,180.

3. Round numbers

You can round numbers to make the initial calculations easier and then subtract or add what was rounded to get the exact answer.

Often times, breaking the calculation into these two steps makes it significantly easier than doing the calculation in one step.

Example*: What is 199 * 35?*

*Instead of multiplying these two numbers, we can round the first number so that we are multiplying 200 * 35.*

*200 * 35 = 7,000.*

Because we rounded 199 to 200, we need to subtract one instance of 35 from our final answer.

7,000 – 35 = 6,965, which is our final answer.

4. Use factors of numbers

You can use factors of numbers to break down an operation into several smaller and more manageable steps.

Example*: What is 115 * 12?*

*Instead of just multiplying these two numbers, it is easier to re-write this as 115 * 6 * 2.*

*115 * 6 = 690.*

*690 * 2 = 1,380.*

By splitting the multiplication into two steps, we can calculate the final answer much more easily and quickly.

5. Reverse percentages

This math tip can be used when multiplying a number with a percentage. You can switch or reverse the percentages to make the calculation easier.

Example: *What is 32% of 25?*

After flipping or reversing the percentages, we can re-write this problem as 25% of 32. Written this way, the answer is much more obvious, 8.

6. Sense check numbers along the way

After each major step of a math calculation, you can do a quick sense check to see if your answer is the right order of magnitude.

Accidentally missing zeroes or adding extra zeroes during your calculations is the most common math mistake. It only takes a few seconds to check this.

Example: *If you are multiplying 125 million by 24, you should expect your answer to be in the billions because 100 million * 20 = 2 billion. You should do a quick sense check after each major calculation before proceeding to the next step.*

Summary

- Estimation questions ask you to estimate a particular number or figure by making assumptions and performing calculations

- One of the most common types of estimation questions are market sizing questions, which ask you to estimate the annual spending of a specific category of product

- For estimation questions, you are evaluated on whether you can take a logical, structured approach and whether you are comfortable dealing with numbers

- There are two methods to tackle estimation questions

    - In a top-down approach, start with a large number and then refine and break down the number until you get your answer

    - In a bottom-up approach, start with a small number and then build up and increase the number until you get your answer

- There are three strategies to make reasonable assumptions:

    - Use personal experiences

    - Use a proxy

    - Use lower and upper bounds

- Follow these estimation math tips to simplify your math calculations and greatly decrease the chances that you make a mistake:

    - Work with units instead of numbers

    - Use the distributive property

- Round numbers
- Use factors of numbers
- Reverse percentages
- Sense check numbers along the way

Practice

1. How many TV ads are shown in the United States each day?

2. What is the market size of electric toothbrushes in the United States?

3. What is the market size of beer in the United States?

4. How many airplanes take off from Los Angeles International Airport (LAX) each day?

5. How many golf balls fit in a standard airplane?

6. What is the length of spaghetti consumed in the United States each year? Use inches for your units.

Solutions

1. How many TV ads are shown in the U.S. each day?

One potential approach could look like the following:

- *Estimate the number of TV channels in the U.S.*
- *Assume each channel is on-air for 24 hours each day*
- *Estimate the percentage of airtime that is given to ads*
- *Estimate the average duration of an ad*
- *Divide total ad airtime by ad duration to determine how many TV ads are shown in the U.S.*

*Starting with the number of TV channels, let's assume there are 2,000 channels. If each channel is on-air for 24 hours each day, that gives us 2,000 * 24 = 48,000 hours of airtime each day.*

*Let's say that ads take up approximately one-fourth of total airtime. Therefore, ads run for 1/4 * 48,000 = 12,000 hours each day.*

The average duration of an ad is estimated to be 30 seconds or 0.5 minutes. 12,000 hours is the equivalent of 720,000 minutes.

So, 720,000 minutes divided by 0.5 minutes per ad gives 1,440,000 TV ads that are shown in the U.S. each day.

2. What is the market size of electric toothbrushes in the U.S.?

Market size is defined as the total dollars of sales of a product or service in one year. One potential approach could be:

- *Start with the U.S. population*
- *Estimate the percentage that brushes their teeth*

- *Estimate the percentage that uses electric toothbrushes*
- *Estimate how many electric toothbrushes the average person purchases each year*
- *Estimate the cost of an electric toothbrush*
- *Multiply all of these figures to determine the market size of electric toothbrushes in the U.S.*

*We'll assume there are roughly 320 million people in the U.S. Assume that 90% of the population brushes their teeth. This leaves us with 320M * 90% = 288M people.*

*Assume that 25% of people use electric toothbrushes. That gives us 288M * 25% = 72M people.*

Let's estimate that a person buys a new electric toothbrush every three years. This means that 72M / 3 = 24M electric toothbrushes are purchased every year.

*If the average electric toothbrush costs $50, then the market size is 24M * $50 = $1.2B.*

3. What is the market size of beer in the United States?

   For this market sizing problem, you could structure your approach in the following way:

   - *Start with the U.S. population*
   - *Estimate the percentage that are legally allowed to drink alcohol*
   - *Estimate the percentage that drink beer*
   - *Estimate the frequency in which people drink beer*
   - *Estimate the average price per can or bottle of beer*

- *Multiply all of these figures to determine the market size of beer in the United States*

We'll assume there are roughly 320 million people in the U.S.

*Assuming the average life expectancy is 80 years and that there is an even distribution of ages, roughly 75% of the population can legally drink alcohol. This gives 320M * 75% = 240M people.*

*Of these people, let's assume 75% drink beer. This gives us 240M * 75% = 180M beer drinks.*

*Assume that a person drinks five beers a week, or roughly 250 beers per year, assuming roughly 50 weeks per year. This gives us 180M * 250 = 45B cans or bottles of beer.*

*Let's say that the average can or bottle of beer costs $2. This gives a market size of 45B * $2 = $90B.*

4. How many airplanes take off from Los Angeles International Airport (LAX) each day?

   One potential structure for this estimation question could look like the following:

   - *Estimate the number of hours in a day when planes can take off from an airport*
   - *Estimate what percentage of takeoff time is high-traffic takeoff vs. low-traffic takeoff*
   - *Estimate the average time between takeoffs during the high-traffic takeoff period and low-traffic takeoff period*
   - *Calculate the number of airplanes that take off from LAX each day*

Let's assume that airplanes can take off from LAX between 6AM and the following 2AM. This gives us 20 hours of takeoff time.

A high volume of takeoffs occurs between 9AM and 5PM, which gives us 8 hours of high-traffic takeoff time. The remaining 12 hours can be considered low-traffic takeoff time.

*During high-traffic takeoff time, let's assume 1 airplane takes off every minute. Therefore, 8 hours * 60 minutes * 1 takeoff per minute = 480 takeoffs.*

*During low-traffic takeoff time, let's assume 1 airplane takes off every 3 minutes. Therefore, 12 hours * 60 minutes * 1/3 takeoffs per minute = 240 take offs.*

Adding these two figures together, 480 takeoffs + 240 takeoffs = 720 takeoffs per day from Los Angeles Airport.

5. How many golf balls fit in a standard airplane?

We need to find the volume of an airplane and divide that by the volume of a golf ball. We can use basic geometry to make these calculations. One simple structure could be the following:

Estimate the volume of an airplane:

- *Model an airplane as a rectangular prism, with volume = length * width * height*
- *Estimate an airplane's length, height, and width*
- *Estimate what percentage of an airplane is empty space vs. space that is occupied by seats*
- *Multiply these figures to determine the volume of an airplane that can fit golf balls*

Estimate the volume of a golf ball

- *Model a golf ball as a sphere, with volume = (4/3) * π * radius*^{3}
- *Estimate the diameter of a golf ball*

- *Convert the diameter to a radius*
- *Calculate the volume of a golf ball*
- *Divide the volume of an airplane by the volume of a golf ball to determine the number of golf balls that will fit*

*Let's start by calculating the volume of an airplane. We can estimate that its length is 100 ft, width is 10 ft, and height is 10 ft. That makes the volume 100 ft * 10 ft * 10 ft = 10,000 cubic feet.*

*Let's assume that 80% of the volume of an airplane is empty space and the remaining 20% is occupied by solid things, such as seats. Therefore, the empty space in an airplane is 80% * 10,000 cubic feet = 8,000 cubic feet.*

Moving onto calculating the volume of a golf ball, we can estimate that the diameter of a golf ball to be about 1.5 inches in diameter. Therefore, the radius is 0.75 inches, half of the diameter.

The volume of a sphere = $(4/3) * \pi * \text{radius}^3$. *So,* $(4/3) * (3.14) * (0.75)^3 = 1.77$ *cubic inches.*

*Next, we'll need to convert from cubic inches to cubic feet. Because there are 12 inches in a foot, that means there are 12 * 12 * 12 cubic inches in a cubic foot. So, 1.77 cubic inches / (12 * 12 * 12) = 0.001 cubic feet. This is the volume of a golf ball in units of cubic feet.*

Finally, we'll divide the volume of an airplane by the volume of a golf ball to get our answer.

8,000 cubic feet / 0.001 cubic feet = 8M golf balls that can fit in a standard airplane.

6. What is the length of spaghetti consumed in the United States each year? Use inches for your units.

Here is one structured approach you could use:

- *Start with the US population*

- *Estimate the percentage of people that eat spaghetti*
- *Segment these people into high-frequency and low-frequency spaghetti consumers*
- *Estimate the frequency in which high-frequency and low-frequency consumers eat spaghetti each year*
- *Calculate the number of spaghetti meals in the US each year*
- *For the average meal, estimate how many bites are taken*
- *For the average bite, estimate how many strands of spaghetti are consumed*
- *Estimate the length of an average strand of spaghetti*
- *Multiply these figures to determine the length of spaghetti consumed in the US each year*

*Starting with a US population size of 320M, let's estimate that 75% of people eat spaghetti. That gives us 75% * 320M = 240M people.*

Among these 240M people, let's estimate that 25% eat spaghetti with high-frequency and 75% eat spaghetti with low-frequency. Therefore, there are 60M high-frequency consumers and 180M low-frequency consumers.

*Let's estimate that high-frequency consumers eat spaghetti three times a week, or about 150 times a year. Therefore, high-frequency consumers account for 60M * 150 = 9B spaghetti meals.*

*Let's estimate that low-frequency consumers eat spaghetti a little less than once a month, or roughly 10 times a year. Therefore, low-frequency consumers account for 180M * 10 = 1.8B spaghetti meals.*

The total number of spaghetti meals is 9B + 1.8B = 10.8B.

*For the average meal, let's assume that 10 bites are needed to finish the meal. In each bite, we'll assume there are 5 spaghetti strands. Therefore, the average meal contains 10 bites * 5 strands per bite = 50 strands of spaghetti.*

*10.8B spaghetti meals * 50 strands of spaghetti per meal = 540B strands of spaghetti.*

The average spaghetti strand length is 10 inches.

*Therefore, the length of spaghetti consumed in the US each year is 540B strands of spaghetti * 10 inches length per strand = 5.4T inches.*

9. Strategy Questions

What are strategy questions?

Strategy questions ask you to make a high-level business decision that could impact the direction of the entire company, not just a single product.

Examples of strategy questions include:

- Should we enter this new geography?
- Should we build this new product?
- How should we respond to a competitor's new product?

Answering strategy questions requires you to take a step back and think more high-level, rather than focusing on specific product features or requirements.

This is important because product managers sometimes get lost in the details and technicalities of specific product features and requirements that they lose sight of the overall goal or objective of the company.

What are interviewers looking for?

There are three major qualities that interviewers are looking for when asking strategy questions:

- **Business acumen**: Do you have a basic understanding of fundamental business concepts? Do your conclusions and recommendations make sense from a business perspective?

- **Structured, logical thinking**: Can you structure complex problems in a clear, simple way? Can you use logic and reason to make appropriate conclusions?

- **Communication skills**: Can you communicate in a clear, concise way? Are you articulate in what you are saying?

How do you answer strategy questions?

When answering a strategy question, you should create a framework to structure your thoughts rather than saying the first few ideas that come to mind.

A framework is a tool to structure and break down business problems into smaller components.

Example: *Should a company based in the United States enter the China market?*

We can break this broad strategy question into four major questions.

- *Is China an attractive market?*

- *Is there heavy competition in China?*

- *Does the company have the capabilities to enter the China market?*

- *Will entering the China market be profitable?*

We can further break these four major questions down into smaller, more manageable questions to answer.

- *Is China an attractive market?*
    - *What is the market size?*
    - *What is the market growth rate?*
    - *What are average profit margins in the market?*
- *Is there heavy competition in China?*
    - *How many competitors are there?*
    - *How much share do they have?*
    - *Do competitors have any competitive advantages?*
- *Does the company have the capabilities to enter the China market?*
    - *Are there significant synergies that the company can leverage?*
    - *Are there any significant capability gaps?*
- *Will entering the China market be profitable?*
    - *What are expected revenues and costs?*
    - *How long will it take to break even?*

The answers to the questions in your framework will help you answer the overall strategy question.

***Example**: Let's say that you believe the following is true:*

- *The China market is massive, growing quickly, and has high average profit margins*

- *The market is highly fragmented, each player has a tiny market share, and no competitor has any competitive advantages*

- *The company has significant synergies they can leverage in China and there are no significant capability gaps*

- *Revenues are expected to be high, costs are expected to be minimal, and the company will break even in a few months*

If this were the case, then you would recommend that the company should enter the China market.

On the other hand, let's say that you believe the following is true:

- *The China market is small, declining rapidly, and has low average profit margins*

- *The market is highly concentrated among a few competitors that have high market share, with each competitor having a distinct competitive advantage*

- *There are minimal synergies that the company can leverage in China and there are major capability gaps*

- *Revenues are expected to be minimal, costs are expected to be high, and the company will take many years to break even*

If this were the case, then you would recommend that the company should not enter the China market.

There are six steps to creating outstanding frameworks to answer strategy questions.

1. Memorize eight robust business categories

2. When asked a strategy question, ask for a few minutes to structure your thoughts

3. Mentally run through the eight business categories and select the 3-4 most relevant ones

4. If you are unable to select 3-4 relevant business categories, think of your own business categories to include

5. Add specific questions under each business category you've selected

6. Walk the interviewer through your framework and answer

1. Memorize eight robust business categories

There are eight broad business categories that are frequently looked at when making strategy decisions.

By memorizing these eight categories, you'll have an easier time creating an outstanding framework rather than having to create frameworks from scratch each time.

These eight business categories are:

- **Market**: market size, market growth rate, average profit margins in the market, market trends or changes (e.g., technology, regulation)

- **Competition**: number of competitors, market share of competitors, competitive advantage of competitors, trends or changes happening among competitors

- **Company**: products and services, strengths, competitive advantages, capability gaps, weaknesses, growth trajectory, synergies

- **Product**: product benefits, product drawbacks, product differentiation, product lifecycle stage

- **Customer**: number of customer segments, characteristics of each segment, attractiveness of each segment, customer needs and preferences, customer purchasing behaviors

- **Profitability**: revenue, costs, breakeven, return on investment, payback period

- **Alternatives**: alternative markets, alternative products, alternative partnerships or strategic alliances, alternative acquisition targets, alternative investments, alternative strategies

- **Risks**: major risks, likelihood of risks, severity of risks, mitigation of risks

For each of these broad business categories, we've included a few potential topics to give you a sense of what each category means or encompasses.

You will only need to memorize the eight broad business categories. You do not need to memorize all of the potential topics under each.

2. Ask for a few minutes to structure your thoughts

When asked a strategy question, ask for a few minutes to structure your thoughts. Almost every time, the interviewer will give you time to develop a framework.

3. Mentally run through the eight business categories

Next, mentally run through the eight business categories that you've memorized and select the 3-4 most relevant ones.

3-4 is the ideal number of categories for your framework. It is the right balance of comprehensiveness and simplicity.

Any fewer than 3-4 categories and your framework may not be comprehensive enough. You may be missing critical questions that are necessary to answer the strategy question.

Any more than 3-4 categories and your framework becomes too large and complicated. You also risk having redundancies in your framework.

4. Think of your own business categories to include

If you are unable to get 3-4 categories in your framework after running through the memorized list of business categories, then it is time to think of your own business categories to include.

This happens more commonly when given atypical or unusual strategy questions.

Remember, the eight broad business categories you memorized work for the vast majority of strategy questions, but does not cover all of them.

5. Add specific questions under each business category

Once you have identified the 3-4 major categories in your framework, add sub-bullets or questions underneath each of them to add more detail.

6. Walk the interviewer through your framework and answer

When you've finished developing your framework, walk your interviewer through it.

At the end of each major category, give your opinion on which answer or recommendation it supports.

Once you've walked the interviewer through your entire framework, you should have an overall answer to the strategy question.

Examples of strategy questions

***Example #1**: Our company operates in the e-commerce space, primarily focusing on fashion and apparel. We're considering building a virtual fitting room feature that allows customers to virtually try on clothing items before making a purchase. How would you approach the decision of whether to invest in and build this new virtual fitting room feature?*

There are four major factors to consider when deciding whether to build this new product feature:

- ***Customer needs and preferences****: Does this product feature resonate with customers?*
    - *Do customers have a need for a virtual fitting room?*
    - *Will customers actually use this feature?*
- ***Company capabilities****: Does our company have the capabilities to develop this product feature?*
    - *Do we have the expertise or technological capabilities to develop this feature?*
    - *Do we have sufficient resources to develop this feature? (e.g., people, time, capital)*
- ***Competition****: Will developing this product feature help distinguish ourselves from competitors?*
    - *Do competitors have a virtual fitting room product feature?*
    - *How good are competitors' virtual fitting rooms? (e.g., user experience, value provided to customers)*
- ***Profitability****: Will building this new product feature be profitable?*
    - *What are the expected costs of developing this product feature?*
    - *What is the expected increase in revenue? (e.g., how much will conversion rate increase, how much will refunds decrease)*

For this example, note that we included a high-level question for each of the business categories we've selected. This is optional.

Doing this sometimes helps make the framework more clear, but other times it may be redundant with the specific questions you have underneath each business category.

***Example #2**: Our company specializes in producing high-end fitness trackers. We've just learned that our main competitor has launched a new fitness tracker with advanced health monitoring features. How would you approach responding to this new competitive threat?*

There are four major factors to consider when deciding how to respond to this new competitive threat:

- ***Competitor product**: What is this new product?*
    - *What is its value proposition?*
    - *What are its key features?*
    - *What are its strengths?*
    - *What are its weaknesses?*
- ***Customer**: How are customers going to respond to this new product?*
    - *What do customers think of the product?*
    - *How are customer expectations going to change?*
    - *How are customer purchasing behaviors going to change?*
- ***Company**: What options do we have to respond?*
    - *Should we improve an existing product?*
    - *Should we create a new product?*
    - *Should we change our marketing strategy?*
    - *Should we change our pricing?*

  - *Should we do nothing?*

- ***Financial implications***: *What are the financial implications of our main competitor launching this new product?*

  - *How much do we expect revenue or market share to decrease by due to the new product?*

  - *What revenue or market share can we achieve if we optimally respond to this competitor?*

Example #3: *Our company manufactures smart home security systems and we've recently launched a new model with advanced AI-powered features. How do we increase our market share and customer base?*

There are four major ways to increase our market share and customer base for this smart home security system product:

- ***Develop targeted marketing***

  - *Identify specific customer segments that are most likely to benefit from the product*

  - *Develop tailored marketing campaigns to highlight the unique advantages of our new model*

- ***Form strategic partnerships***

  - *Form partnerships with prominent players in the smart home ecosystem*

  - *Integrate the security system seamlessly into broader home automation solutions*

- ***Enhance customer experience and advocacy***

  - *Prioritize exceptional customer support and post-purchase experience*

  - *Implement a referral program to encourage existing customers to refer friends and family*

- ***Engage with the community***

  - *Actively participate in online communities, forums, and social media groups focused on smart home technology and security*

  - *Provide valuable insights and thought leadership at major smart home conferences or conventions*

For this example, note that we had to think of our own business categories since the memorized list of categories only yielded one category that we could use, customer.

Summary

- A framework is a tool to structure and break down business problems into smaller components
- There are six steps to creating outstanding frameworks to answer strategy questions
    - Memorize eight robust business categories: market, competition, company, product, customer, profitability, alternatives, and risks
    - When asked a business strategy question, ask for a few minutes to structure your thoughts
    - Mentally run through the eight business categories and select the 3-4 most relevant ones
    - If you are unable to select 3-4 relevant business categories, think of your own business categories to include
    - Add specific questions under each business category you've selected
    - Walk the interviewer through your framework and answer

Practice

1. Our company specializes in producing premium athletic footwear. There's an opportunity to enter the outdoor adventure footwear market. How would you approach the decision of whether to invest in and enter this new market?

2. Our company specializes in manufacturing cutting-edge electric vehicles. We're considering forming a strategic partnership with a leading environmental non-profit organization. The partnership aims to collaborate on sustainability initiatives and promote eco-friendly practices. How would you approach the decision of whether to form this partnership?

3. Our company has been manufacturing a range of organic skincare products for several years. However, recent market analysis suggests a shift in consumer preferences towards minimalist skincare routines and natural ingredients. What factors would you consider in deciding whether to discontinue this product line?

4. Our company provides checking and savings accounts, investment accounts, loans, and credit cards to both businesses and individuals in the United States. We are trying to increase revenues and want to enter a foreign country. What should we consider when selecting which country to enter?

5. Our software company has recently been experiencing a decline in profits. How should we determine what is causing this issue and what we should do to address this?

6. Our company is a large social media platform company. We are considering acquiring an online gaming company to incorporate online games into our social media platform. What factors should we consider in deciding whether to make this acquisition?

Solutions

1. Our company specializes in producing premium athletic footwear. There's an opportunity to enter the outdoor adventure footwear market. How would you approach the decision of whether to invest in and enter this new market?

   There are four major considerations in deciding whether to enter the outdoor adventure footwear market.

   - ***Market attractiveness***: *Is the outdoor adventure footwear market attractive?*
     - *What is the market size?*
     - *What is the growth rate?*
     - *What are average profit margins?*
   - ***Competition***: *Is there heavy competition?*
     - *How many competitors are there?*
     - *Do competitors have any competitive advantages?*
   - ***Company capabilities***: *Does our company have the capabilities to produce and sell outdoor adventure footwear?*
     - *Does our company have the knowledge or expertise to create a great product?*
     - *Do we have the right distribution channels to reach customers?*
     - *Are there significant synergies we can leverage with our existing business?*
   - ***Profitability***: *Will entering the outdoor adventure footwear market be profitable?*

- *What are expected revenues?*
- *What are expected costs?*
- *How long will it take for our company to break even?*

2. Our company specializes in manufacturing cutting-edge electric vehicles. We're considering forming a strategic partnership with a leading environmental non-profit organization. The partnership aims to collaborate on sustainability initiatives and promote eco-friendly practices. How would you approach the decision of whether to form this partnership?

   There are four major considerations in deciding whether to form this partnership.

   - ***Customer***
     - *Do customers value sustainability initiatives and eco-friendly practices?*
     - *What will customers think of this partnership?*
     - *How will customer purchasing habits change?*
   - ***Competition***
     - *Do competitors have any partnerships with environmental non-profit organizations?*
     - *If so, how have these partnerships worked out for our competitors?*
   - ***Company***
     - *What does our company expect to gain from this partnership?*

  - *Is our company a good fit for this partnership?*

- ***Financial implications***
  - *What are the costs of entering into this strategic partnership?*
  - *What is the expected increase in revenue from entering into this strategic partnership?*

3. Our company has been manufacturing a range of organic skincare products for several years. However, recent market analysis suggests a shift in consumer preferences towards minimalist skincare routines and natural ingredients. What factors would you consider in deciding whether to discontinue this product line?

   There are four major factors to consider:

- ***Organic skincare product***
  - *What are revenues for our organic skincare products?*
  - *What are growth rates for our organic skincare products?*
  - *What are profit margins for our organic skincare products?*
- ***Customer***
  - *Do customers like our organic skincare products?*
  - *What are our customers' needs and preferences?*
- ***Alternatives***
  - *Can we improve our organic skincare products?*

    - *Can we launch new minimalist skincare products with natural ingredients?*

- ***Financial implications***

    - *What are the costs of maintaining or improving our organic skincare product lines?*
    - *What are the costs of discontinuing our organic skincare product lines?*
    - *What are the costs of launching new minimalist skincare products with natural ingredients?*

4. Our company provides checking and savings accounts, investment accounts, loans, and credit cards to both businesses and individuals in the United States. We are trying to increase revenues and want to enter a foreign country. What should we consider when selecting which country to enter?

   There are four major considerations:

    - ***Attractiveness of each country***

        - *What is the market size in each country?*
        - *What is the market growth rate in each country?*
        - *What are average market profit margins in each country?*

    - ***Competitiveness in each country***

        - *How many players are in each country?*
        - *How concentrated are players in each country?*
        - *How high are barriers to entry in each country?*

- ***Our company's ability to execute in each country***
    - *How strong are our capabilities in each country?*
    - *Can we better leverage synergies in certain countries over others?*
- ***Expected profitability in each country***
    - *What are the expected revenues in each country?*
    - *What are the expected costs in each country?*
    - *How long would it take for us to break even in each country?*

5. Our software company has recently been experiencing a decline in profits. How should we determine what is causing this issue and what we should do to address this?

   There are four major factors to consider:

- ***Drivers of profit***
    - *Has there been a decline in revenue?*
        - *Have sales gone down?*
        - *Have prices gone down?*
    - *Has there been an increase in costs?*
        - *Have variable costs increased?*
        - *Have fixed costs increased?*
- ***Customer needs and preferences***
    - *Have customer needs changed?*

- *Have customers changed their purchasing habits?*
- *Do customers view our company differently?*

- ***Competitors***
    - *Have new competitors entered the market?*
    - *Have existing competitors made any recent strategic moves or changes?*

- ***Software market trends***
    - *Are there new technologies impacting the market?*
    - *Are there new regulations impacting the market?*

6. Our company is a large social media platform company. We are considering acquiring an online gaming company to incorporate online games into our social media platform. What factors should we consider in deciding whether to make this acquisition?

   There are five major factors to consider when deciding whether to make this acquisition:

- ***Online gaming market attractiveness***
    - *What is the market size?*
    - *What is the market growth rate?*
    - *What are average profit margins for this market?*

- ***Online gaming competitive landscape***
    - *How many online gaming companies are there?*
    - *How much share does each company have?*

  - *Do other players have any competitive advantages or differentiation?*

- ***Acquisition target attractiveness***

  - *Is the acquisition target profitable?*

  - *How much market share does the target have?*

  - *Does the acquisition target have any differentiation or competitive advantages?*

  - *Does the target give our company significant revenue or cost synergies?*

- ***Customer considerations***

  - *Do our customers have a need for online gaming on our social media platform?*

  - *What will customers think of this acquisition?*

  - *How will this acquisition change customer preferences or behaviors?*

- ***Financial considerations***

  - *Is the acquisition price fair and reasonable?*

  - *By how much will our company be able to improve and grow the acquisition target?*

  - *What is the expected return on this acquisition?*

10. Metrics Questions

What are metrics questions?

Metrics questions ask you to determine what metrics you would look at when analyzing the performance of a product, feature, or business decision.

For these questions, you should be familiar with what a key performance indicator is.

A key performance indicator, or KPI for short, is a measurable value that evaluates the performance of a company, product, or individual over time. It provides a quantifiable and objective measure of success or progress towards a goal.

While all KPIs are metrics, not all metrics are KPIs. KPIs are a subset of metrics that are specifically chosen for their important relevance to organizational goals and strategic objectives.

Selecting an appropriate and effective KPI to measure a product's success can be challenging and complicated.

***Example**: You are the PM for YouTube. What metric would you look at to measure success?*

For this example, let's define success as the level of usage of YouTube.

Initially, you may think of measuring the number of YouTube users over the past month.

However, the number of users may vary month-to-month due to seasonality. Certain months may naturally have higher viewership than others due to holidays and more leisure time.

Therefore, a better metric may be to measure the number of YouTube users over the past year to remove any effects of seasonality.

Although this is a better metric, not all customers are the same. Some customers may use YouTube once a year while others might use YouTube once a day.

Therefore, you may want to look at the number of YouTube sessions instead of the number of YouTube users. A session can be defined as any instance in which a user visits YouTube.

Still, this metric has an issue. Not all sessions are the same. Some sessions may last for a minute while other sessions may last an hour.

A better metric could be the total number of minutes spent watching videos on YouTube over the past year. The higher this metric is, the more successful YouTube is.

What are interviewers looking for?

Metrics questions are designed to assess your ability to use data and KPIs to make informed decisions and measure the success of a product.

To answer metrics questions successfully, you should display the following three key skills and qualities:

- **Analytical thinking**: the ability to understand and interpret data to drive meaningful insights
- **Understanding of KPIs:** familiarity with relevant KPIs for the product and industry and understanding of how to measure and track them
- **Prioritization**: understanding which metrics are most critical for the product's success

What metrics should you be familiar with?

Although there are thousands of potential metrics that you could measure and use, there are a select few that are especially common for product management.

You should be familiar with the following KPIs:

- **Customer acquisition cost (CAC)**: The cost of acquiring a new customer. It includes all sales and marketing expenses
- **Conversion rate**: The percentage of users who complete a desired action, such as making a purchase or signing up for a newsletter
- **Customer lifetime value (CLTV)**: The predicted net profit generated from a customer over the course of their lifetime. It helps understand the long-term value of a customer
- **Average revenue per user (ARPU)**: The average amount of revenue generated from each user
- **Churn rate**: The percentage of customers that stop using or paying for a product over a specified period of time. High churn rates typically signal customer dissatisfaction

- **Retention rate**: The percentage of customers who continue using the product over a specified period of time. High retention rates typically signal customer satisfaction

- **Yearly, monthly, and daily active users: (YAU, MAU, DAU)**: The number of unique users who engage with the product in a given year, month, or day

- **Net Promoter Score (NPS)**: A measure of customer satisfaction and loyalty. It is calculated as the percentage of promoters (those who are highly satisfied and would recommend the product) minus the percentage of detractors (those who are dissatisfied or unhappy)

However, don't feel that you have to use these metrics when you answer metrics questions. You should try to identify and define your own metric that best measures success.

How do you answer metrics questions?

There are three steps to answer metrics questions:

1. Identify which qualities are most important

2. Brainstorm potential metrics for each quality

3. Select metrics that are accurate and feasibly measured

Let's take a look at an example.

***Example #1**: Quora is a question-and-answer website where questions are asked, answered, and edited by internet users. What metrics can Quora use to identify spam?*

To determine the best metrics, let's first look at the distinguishing characteristics of spam.

One characteristic is that spam posts repeat the same messages and wording. A useful metric to detect spam would be to measure the similarity of a new post with each existing post on Quora. If the latest post is almost identical to an existing one, then it is likely spam.

A second characteristic is that spammers typically copy and paste messages into Quora's text box instead of typing them directly. One potential metric would be to measure the time it takes for a user to submit a post once they begin typing. However, this could be a poor metric because many legitimate Quora users type their answers in a separate word document before transferring them to Quora.

A third characteristic is that spammers post many times in a short period. A helpful metric to detect spam would be to measure how frequently a user has made a post. If the frequency is very high, the user could be a spammer. However, there is a risk of incorrectly detecting spammers because some legitimate Quora users are very productive at answering many questions in a short period.

A fourth characteristic is that spam postings typically come from newer accounts. Monitoring account age can help identify spam.

In summary, creating a metric that measures the similarity of a new post with each existing post would be the most effective metric to identify spam. Metrics measuring the number of posts per hour for new accounts that are less than three weeks old could also be used to supplement this metric.

Example #2: *You are a product manager for a social media platform. How would you measure the effectiveness of a new feature designed to increase user engagement?*

To assess the effectiveness of the new feature aimed at boosting user engagement, we should look at several key metrics:

1. User Engagement Rate (UER):

This metric quantifies the level of interaction users have with the platform. It can be calculated by dividing the total number of engaged actions (likes, comments, shares) by the total number of active users within a specific time period.

For the new feature, we would compare the UER before and after its implementation. An increase in UER indicates that the feature has had a positive impact on user engagement.

2. Session Duration and Frequency:

Analyzing how long users spend on the platform per session and how frequently they visit can provide insights into their level of engagement. If the new feature encourages longer sessions or more frequent visits, it indicates increased user engagement.

3. User Retention Rate:

This metric gauges the percentage of users who continue to use the platform over time. It can be measured over different time intervals (e.g., weekly, monthly).

If the introduction of the new feature leads to higher user retention rates, it suggests that overall user engagement has increased.

4. Feedback and Sentiment Analysis:

Gathering direct user feedback through surveys, comments, and sentiment analysis tools can offer qualitative insights into how users perceive the new feature. Positive sentiment and constructive feedback are indicators of successful engagement.

In summary, by closely monitoring these metrics and conducting regular A/B testing, we can gain a comprehensive understanding of the impact of the new feature on user engagement.

It's important to note that a combination of both quantitative and qualitative metrics provides a well-rounded view of the feature's effectiveness.

Summary

- Metrics questions ask you to determine what metrics you would look at when analyzing the performance of a product, feature, or business decision

- A key performance indicator, or KPI for short, is a measurable value that evaluates the performance of a company, product, or individual over time

- Some of the most common KPIs for product managers include:

    - Customer acquisition cost (CAC)
    - Conversion rate
    - Customer lifetime value (CLV)
    - Average revenue per user (ARPU)
    - Churn rate
    - Retention rate
    - Yearly/monthly/daily active users (YAU, MAU, DAU)
    - Net Promoter Score (NPS)

- There are three steps to answering metrics questions

    - Identify which qualities are most important
    - Brainstorm potential metrics for each quality
    - Select metrics that are accurate and feasibly measured

Practice

1. Airbnb is launching a new feature, "5-star listing." This feature would indicate which listings have at least a 4.8 rating. How would you assess the impact of this feature?

2. Spotify is a digital music service that gives users access to millions of songs for a monthly or annual subscription fee. Name five key performance indicators for Spotify.

3. You are a product manager for Google Search. What are the most important metrics to measure and monitor?

4. You are a product manager for Amazon Web Services, an on-demand cloud computing platform. What are the most important metrics to measure and monitor?

5. You are a product manager for a popular tax preparation software to file taxes online. What are the most important metrics to measure and monitor?

6. You are a product manager for UPS, a package delivery company. What are the most important metrics to measure and monitor?

Solutions

1. Airbnb is launching a new feature, "5-star listing." This feature would indicate which listings have at least a 4.8 rating. How would you assess the impact of this feature?

   We can assess how this feature impacts hosts, guests, and Airbnb's bottom line.

   For hosts, we hope that this feature would make them happier and stay on the platform. To measure this, we can look at how the net promoter score of hosts has changed since the launch of this feature.

   We can also look at how the number of monthly active hosts has changed. An active host can be defined as someone that lists their property in a given month.

   For guests, this feature should make booking selection easier. We can measure the time it takes for a guest to search through listings and make a booking. We can also measure the booking rate for guests, which is the percentage of site visits that lead to a booking.

   For Airbnb, we want to see if this feature increases revenues. The number of monthly bookings can measure this. We could also measure the average booking value since five-star listings could be priced higher due to their perceived quality.

   The goal of this feature is to keep hosts happy and to make bookings easier for guests. Therefore, the two most important metrics to measure are host net promoter score and guest booking rate.

2. Spotify is a digital music service that gives users access to millions of songs for a monthly or annual subscription fee. Name five key performance indicators for Spotify and what data you would use.

   The most important qualities Spotify should measure are user growth and user engagement. If Spotify has high user growth and high user engagement, then they are likely performing well.

One, we can look at monthly active users and how it changes over time. This will give a sense of how many current users Spotify has and whether it is growing or shrinking. An active user can be defined as a user that has opened the app at least once in a given month.

Two, we can look at the change in the number of new users for each month. The number of new users can be defined as the number of new accounts created. This will give a measure of Spotify's new customer growth rate.

Three, for a previous month, we can compare how many active users last month are still active this month. This will give a measure of Spotify's existing user attrition rate.

Four, we can look at the number of monthly app opens. This will measure how frequently users engage with Spotify.

Five, we can look at the monthly duration of app usage. This will give us a measure of how long users engage with Spotify each month.

3. You are a product manager for Google Search. What are the most important metrics to measure and monitor?

   A few key metrics include the following:

   - *Search volume: The total number of searches conducted. This metric helps assess the popularity and relevance of the search engine*
   - *Bounce rate: The percentage of users who leave the search results page without clicking on any result. A high bounce rate may indicate that users aren't finding what they need*
   - *Click-through rate (CTR): The percentage of users who click on a search result after seeing it. A high CTR indicates that users find the search results relevant, while a low CTR indicates that the results are not meeting user expectations*

- *Dwell time: The amount of time a user spends on a page after clicking through the search results. Longer dwell times indicate that users are finding the content valuable*

- *Search load time: Faster search load times contribute to a better user experience. Monitoring and optimizing the speed at which search results pages load can impact user satisfaction*

4. You are a product manager for Amazon Web Services, an on-demand cloud computing platform. What are the most important metrics to measure and monitor?

   A few key metrics include the following:

   - *Uptime / availability: The percentage of time the cloud computing platform is up and running. Downtime can have significant impacts on users and their applications*

   - *Latency: The time it takes for data to travel between its source and destination. Low latency is critical for providing responsive and high-performance services*

   - *Resource utilization: Understanding how resources (e.g., storage, databases) are utilized. This helps optimize costs while ensuring customer needs are met*

   - *Network throughput: The amount of data transferred over the network. This helps ensure efficient data delivery and identify potential bottlenecks*

   - *Incident response metrics: The time it takes to detect and respond to incidents. This helps ensure a prompt and effective response to any issues that may arise*

5. You are a product manager for a popular tax preparation software to file taxes online. What are the most important metrics to measure and monitor?

   A few key metrics include the following:

- *Filing rate: The percentage of users who complete the entire tax filing process. This helps measure the effectiveness of the user interface and overall user experience*

- *Completion time: The average time it takes for users to complete their tax filings. A streamlined and efficient process is likely to result in shorter completion times and improved user satisfaction*

- *Error rates: The frequency of errors in tax filings. High error rates may indicate issues with the software's usability or the need for clearer instructions*

- *User retention rate: The percentage of users who continue to use the software over time. High retention rates indicate high user satisfaction and likelihood of repeat business*

- *Upgrades and cross-selling metrics: Tracking the adoption of upgrades and cross-selling success to maximize revenue*

6. You are a product manager for UPS, a package delivery company. What are the most important metrics to measure and monitor?

   A few key metrics include the following:

   - *On-time delivery rate: The percentage of packages that are delivered on or before the expected delivery date. This is a crucial metric for customer satisfaction and reflects the reliability of the company's delivery services*

   - *Delivery cost per package: The costs associated with delivering each package. Monitoring this metric helps optimize operational efficiency and control costs*

   - *Lost or damaged packages: The incidence of lost or damaged packages. Minimizing these occurrences is critical for customer satisfaction and operational efficiency*

- *Delivery time predictability: The percentage of delivery time estimates that align with the actual delivery times. Predictable delivery times contribute to customer satisfaction and trust*

- *Delivery attempts: The number of delivery attempts per package. A high number of failed delivery attempts may indicate issues with address accuracy or customer availability*

Bonus Tip: You can look at a company's financial reports or press releases to see what metrics are mentioned. These are likely the most important metrics that the company measures and monitors.

11. Execution Questions

What are execution questions?

Execution questions ask what you would do in a particular situation or scenario as the product manager. They are asked to assess how you would react or respond to common types of problems PMs face on a daily basis.

There are three common types of execution questions:

- Investigating a metric
- A/B testing questions
- Optimizing a flow or funnel

What are interviewers looking for?

There are three major skills and qualities that interviewers look for when asking execution questions:

- **Structured, logical thinking**: Can you organize your thinking and approach in a clear, structured way? Can you use logic to draw appropriate conclusions?

- **Analytical problem solving**: Can you break down a complex problem into smaller components? Can you effectively use data to drive decision-making?

- **Adaptability**: Can you adapt your approach to problem solving when faced with new challenges or information? Can you respond to changes quickly?

To answer execution questions well, it is helpful to become familiar with strategies and techniques that PMs actually use on the job. We'll cover all the essentials you need to know for each type of execution question.

Investigating a metric

This type of execution question asks what you would do or how you would respond if you find out that a particular metric has either increased or decreased in an undesired way.

For example:

- The number of visits to our website this March has decreased by 10% compared to February. What should we do?

- Our customer acquisition cost has increased by 30% this quarter. What is going on?

- The number of customer cancellations has tripled this week compared to the prior week. Why is this happening?

There are six steps to efficiently investigate a metric.

Step 1: Compare against the right historical data

The first step when investing a metric anomaly is to compare it to the right historical data to see if it is actually an issue.

Example: *The number of visits to our website this March has decreased by 10% compared to February. What should we do?*

Comparing website visits for the month of March against website visits for the month of February is not the fairest comparison.

Since February and March are two different months, there may be some effects of seasonality that naturally cause differences in website visits.

Therefore, it might make more sense to compare website visits in March to website visits in March of the previous year.

In this example, let's say that website visits this March has actually decreased by 30% compared to last March.

Step 2: Check against competitors or the industry

The next step when investigating a metric anomaly is to see if competitors or the industry overall is also seeing this anomaly.

This will help you deduce whether the issue is a company-specific issue or an industry-wide issue.

Example: *If your company's website traffic in March has decreased by 30%, but your competitors are seeing a 10% increase in traffic, then this issue appears to be an issue specific to your company.*

Step 3: Look at the metric by different segments

The next step is to look at the metric by different segments to see if there is a particular segment that is driving the majority of the anomaly.

Common ways of segmenting a metric are by:

- Geography: segmenting by country, region, city, state, or specific stores
- Product: segmenting by product offering
- Customer demographics: segmenting by age, gender, or income
- Customer lifecycle: segmenting by new customer or returning customer
- Customer behavior: segmenting by purchase history, engagement level, or browsing habits
- Channel: segmenting by in-store sales, mobile app, or online visit
- Industry: segmenting customers based on the industry they serve (e.g., healthcare, finance, technology)
- Time period: segmenting by day, week, month, quarter, or year

Example: *Let's say that you segment the website traffic metric by country. You notice that most countries have seen a 10% increase in traffic, but Brazil has seen a 100% drop in traffic.*

Step 4: Identify the root cause of the issue

Once you have identified the specific segment that is driving the majority of the anomaly, you can dive deeper into understanding what the root cause is.

It can be helpful to think about the product, its intended customers, and their pain points to brainstorm potential causes of the issue.

Example: *There are a few potential reasons why Brazil is seeing a 100% drop in website traffic:*

- *There are technical issues in Brazil with our servers or hosting*

- *Brazil has had electricity outages*
- *Brazil has had internet connectivity problems*
- *The government of Brazil has banned our website*

Let's say that for this example, there have been technical issues in Brazil with our servers or hosting during the month of March. It has since been resolved.

Step 5: Brainstorm potential solutions

Once you've identified the root cause of the issue, you can brainstorm potential solutions. Ideally try to brainstorm at least three different ideas.

You can then assess which solution is best by assessing their impact, ease of implementation, and cost.

Example: *There are multiple potential solutions for technical server and hosting issues in Brazil. We can perform regular server health checks to prevent the issue from occurring, switch to a different host, or have backup servers or hosting in place.*

We might want to recommend the third solution because if the primary servers and hosting goes down, backup servers and hosting can keep the website online.

Step 6: Propose a plan to test or implement your solution

For solutions that have significant costs or risks, it is best practice to propose a plan to test your solution before rolling it out across the entire organization.

Example: *To see if having backup servers and hosting works effectively, we can roll this out to a single major city in Brazil, such as São Paulo or Rio de Janeiro. If the solution works effectively, we can roll it out to the rest of Brazil and even other countries that are prone to having technical server or hosting issues.*

A/B testing questions

This type of execution question asks how you would test the success of a particular product feature or requirement.

For example:

- You are launching a new feature on your platform and want to ensure that it is well-received by users. How would you test this?

- You are the PM for an e-commerce website. You want to improve the click-through rate (CTR) on a particular product page. How would you structure an experiment to achieve this goal?

- You have just launched a major redesign of your app's user interface. How would you go about measuring the impact of this change?

Experimentation is a critical tool in the product manager toolkit. The most commonly run experimental test is called an A/B test.

What is A/B testing?

A/B testing, also known as split testing, is an approach used in experimental design to evaluate the effectiveness of two or more versions of a variable against a specific goal or metric.

Examples of variables can be different web pages, marketing emails, or product features.

The goal of A/B testing is to objectively compare different versions of a variable to determine which one performs better in achieving a predefined goal.

By isolating the variable of interest and randomly assigning participants to different test groups, the results of the different versions of a variable can be observed.

How do you design an A/B test?

There are five steps to design an A/B test.

Step 1: Define your objective and hypothesis

The first step in designing an A/B test is to define a specific objective that you want to achieve.

Example: *We want to increase the click-through rate (CTR) on a call-to-action button on our website.*

Once an objective is defined, formulate a hypothesis that you want to test. A hypothesis is an educated guess on how a proposed change in a particular element will affect a measurable outcome.

Example: *Changing the color of the call-to-action button from green to blue will result in a different CTR.*

Step 2: Identify your variable and versions

The variable is the element that you want to test. You will need to create two or more variations of the variable to be tested.

Example: *Our variable in this example is the color of the call-to-action button. There are two versions of it, a green button and a blue button.*

Step 3: Determine sample size

Next, we need to calculate the sample size needed for the experiment. There needs to be a high enough sample size in order to detect meaningful differences between the versions.

There is quite a bit of statistical knowledge you need to know in order to calculate the minimum sample size needed in an experiment.

We'll provide a brief overview below on how you would calculate the minimum sample size needed by hand. However, you should know that most PMs use online tools or calculators to help them with this.

It is very unlikely that you'll ever need to calculate the sample size needed by hand in an interview, but it is helpful to at least have a high-level understanding of how it works.

To calculate the sample size needed, we need to define:

- The significance level (α): the probability of concluding that there is a significant effect or difference in the data when there actually isn't. This is typically set at 0.05

- Power level (1- β): the probability of detecting a true effect or difference when one actually exists. This is typically set at 0.8

- Mean of the control group: the average value observed in the control group

- Mean of the treatment group: the expected average value in the treatment group

- Standard deviation of the control group: the amount of variation or dispersion from the mean in the control group

- Standard deviation of the treatment group: the expected amount of variation or dispersion from the mean in the treatment group

We can then input these values into a statistical formula that calculates the minimum sample size needed.

$$n = (\sigma_1^2 + \sigma_2^2)\left(z_{1-\frac{\alpha}{2}} + z_{1-\beta}\right)^2 / (\mu_2 - \mu_1)^2$$

This formula is for a two-sided test. It is called a two-sided test because it tests both:

- If the mean of the treatment group is significantly greater than the mean of the control group

- If the mean of the treatment group is significantly less than the mean of the control group

In this equation:

- $n = sample\ size\ needed\ for\ each\ group$

- $\mu_1 = mean\ of\ group\ 1$

- $\mu_2 = mean\ of\ group\ 2$

- $\sigma_1 = standard\ deviation\ of\ group\ 1$

- $\sigma_2 = standard\ deviation\ of\ group\ 2$

- $\alpha = significance\ level$

- $1 - \beta = power\ level$

- $z = critical\ value\ of\ the\ Normal\ distribution$

If you are doing this calculation by hand, you'll need a special z-score table in order to look up the critical values in the formula.

Example: *Let's define the following for this A/B test:*

- *Significance level (a) = 0.05*

- *Power level (1- β) = 0.80*

- *Mean of control group = 10% or 0.1*

- *Expected mean of treatment group = 12% or 0.12*

- *Standard deviation of control group = 0.05*

- *Standard deviation of treatment group = 0.05 (assumed to be the same as the control group)*

Plugging these values into the formula for minimum sample size, we get ≈ 99 participants.

Therefore, we need at least 99 participants in both the control and treatment group to have the desired level of significance and power.

Step 4: Randomly assign participants

Next, we need to randomly assign users or participants to the different versions.

Randomization is critical for A/B testing because it reduces the influence of biases and external factors or variables. This allows for a more valid comparison between control and treatment groups.

Example: *Let's define Group A as the green call-to-action button. This is the current color of the call-to-action button, so this group is the control group.*

Let's define Group B as the blue call-to-action button. This is the new color that we are testing, so this group is the treatment group.

We need to randomly assign participants into Group A and Group B such that each group has at least 99 participants.

Step 5: Set up data tracking

Before running the experiment, it's important to implement any necessary tools or techniques to collect and record the relevant metrics that will be used to evaluate the performance of the different versions of the variable.

Example: *For this A/B test, we will need to ensure we are tracking the number of views and clicks each button color gets in order to calculate the CTR.*

How do you analyze the results of an A/B test?

After the experiment has been run for a sufficient amount of time to gather enough data, we can compare the performance metrics between the different groups.

We can use statistical tests to determine if the observed differences are statistically significant. Statistical significance indicates that the observed difference in data is unlikely to have occurred by chance.

Example: *Let's say that we observe the following from our A/B test:*

- $\mu_1 = 0.10$
- $\mu_2 = 0.11$
- $\sigma_1 = 0.05$
- $\sigma_2 = 0.05$

We can plug these values into an online calculator to see if the difference in means is statistically significant.

To check for statistical significance, we need to calculate something called a p-value and compare it to our significance level (a).

A p-value, or probability value, is a measure that determines the evidence against a statement of no effect or no difference.

If the p-value is less than our significance level, then our results are statistically significant. If the p-value is greater than our significance level, then our results are not statistically significant.

Plugging these values into an online calculator, we see that the p-value is greater than our significance level of 0.05.

Therefore, the results of this A/B test are not statistically significant. Even though the treatment group had a 11% conversion compared to our control group that saw a 10% conversion, we were unable to prove that this was not due to chance.

Optimizing a flow or funnel

This type of execution question asks you to optimize a linear sequence of steps that a customer goes through in order to achieve a particular goal or objective.

***Example**: let's say that we are trying to increase sales on our website. A typical customer funnel might look something like this:*

- *Customer visits website*
- *Customer signs up for the company's email newsletter*
- *Customer receives and opens a marketing email*
- *Customer clicks on a product link in the marketing email*
- *Customer adds the product to their cart*
- *Customer checks out and purchases the product*

There are four steps to optimize a flow or funnel.

Step 1: Identify all of the steps in a customer flow

The first step in optimizing a flow or funnel is to identify all of the different steps.

A helpful way to do this is to imagine that you are the user or customer. Imagine the exact steps you would go through in order to reach the ultimate end goal or objective.

This will help make your list comprehensive. You don't want to miss any steps in this process or else your analysis will not be thorough enough.

Also, make sure each step encompasses just one action done by the user or customer. Don't combine several actions into one step because it will make your analysis more complicated.

***Example**: Let's list out all of the steps in the customer journey when a customer sees an online ad to purchase a particular product.*

- *Customer sees online ad →*
- *Customer clicks on ad →*
- *Customer browses the product page →*
- *Customer adds the product to cart →*
- *Customer starts checkout →*
- *Customer completes checkout*

Step 2: Identify which steps are underperforming

Once you have a comprehensive list of steps in the user or customer flow, the next step is to identify which steps are underperforming.

There are two different ways to identify the steps that are underperforming.

The first way is to look at the conversion rates of each step and see which conversion rates are lowest. These are the steps that you will want to improve.

The second way is to look at the conversion rates of each step, but compare them to industry benchmarks. The steps that are significantly below industry benchmarks are the ones that you will want to improve.

***Example**: Suppose you measure the conversion rates of each of the steps in this customer journey:*

- *Customer clicks on ad → (10%)*
- *Customer browses the page → (50%)*
- *Customer adds the product to cart → (5%)*

- *Customer starts checkout → (40%)*
- *Customer completes checkout → (60%)*

Based on this, the lowest conversion rates occur when the customer clicks on the ad and when the customer adds a product to cart. These could be important steps to focus on improving.

However, suppose you were able to get industry benchmarks on each of the steps:

- *Customer clicks on ad → (10%, benchmark: 5%)*
- *Customer browses the page → (50%, benchmark: 50%)*
- *Customer adds the product to cart → (5%, benchmark: 2%)*
- *Customer starts checkout → (40%, benchmark: 50%)*
- *Customer completes checkout → (60%, benchmark: 80%)*

Based on these benchmarks, the conversion rates of the customer clicking on the ad and the customer adding the product to cart are actually high. They perform better than the industry benchmarks.

The lowest performing steps are actually when the customer starts checkout and when the customer completes checkout.

Step 3: Brainstorm potential solutions

Once you've identified the steps that are underperforming, you can brainstorm potential solutions. Ideally try to brainstorm at least three different ideas.

You can then assess which solution is best by assessing their impact, ease of implementation, and cost.

Example*: To improve the conversion rate of the customer completing checkout we can:*

- *Reduce the number of fields the customer has to fill in to complete checkout*

- *Reduce the number of buttons the customer needs to click to complete the checkout process*

- *Make the checkout page easier to read*

- *Remove any links on the checkout pages so that the customer cannot return to other webpages*

- *Offer the customer a discount code that has a short expiration time on the checkout screen to incentivize checkout completion*

Step 4: Propose a plan to test or implement your solution

For solutions that have significant costs or risks, it is best practice to propose a plan to test your solution before rolling it out across the entire organization.

Example: *Suppose you are interested in offering a discount code that has a short expiration time on the checkout screen. You believe that the increase in checkout completion rate will make up for the decrease in revenues due to the discount.*

Rather than launching this feature on your website to all customers, you may want to launch it for a smaller subset of customers to ensure that it is profitable.

If the checkout completion rate does not increase significantly, then this feature should not be added to the website.

Summary

- Execution questions ask what you would do in a particular situation or scenario as the product manager
- There are three common types of execution questions:
    - Investigating a metric
    - A/B testing questions
    - Optimizing a flow or funnel
- To answer questions on investigating a metric:
    - Compare against the right historical data
    - Check against competitors or the industry
    - Look at the metric by different segments
    - Identify the root cause of the issue
    - Brainstorm potential solutions
    - Propose a plan to test or implement your solution
- To answer A/B testing questions:
    - Define your objective and hypothesis
    - Identify your variable and versions
    - Determine sample size
    - Randomly assign participants
    - Set up data tracking
    - Analyze the results of the A/B test

- To answer questions on optimizing a flow or funnel:
    - Identify all of the steps in a customer flow
    - Identify which steps are underperforming
    - Brainstorm potential solutions
    - Propose a plan to test or implement your solution

Practice

1. You are a product manager for an e-commerce platform's mobile app. Recently, you've noticed a significant drop in the conversion rate for product listings. What steps would you take to address this issue and improve the conversion rate for the mobile app?

2. Imagine that you are the product manager for a recipe-sharing website. Recently, watch time for our cooking video tutorials has been lower than expected. You believe that viewers are increasingly preferring shorter-form content that is much more concise and engaging. All videos currently on the website are between 8-10 minutes.

   Design an A/B test to address this issue and test whether incorporating more shorter-form content would increase overall watch time.

3. You are the product manager at a subscription-based meditation app that offers a 3-day free trial followed by a monthly subscription. With a free trial, users can complete one meditation session per day. The company has observed a drop in conversion rates from the free trial to paid subscriptions. How would you go about optimizing the user flow to increase the conversion rate from trial users to paying subscribers?

4. As a product manager for a music streaming service, you notice a decline in user retention rates. What steps would you take to investigate and address this issue?

5. What are different ways of increasing checkout conversion? Propose a potential A/B test setup to assess the impact of each.

6. Identify the different steps a customer goes through when purchasing a new car. How could you improve each step to increase the likelihood that a customer purchases a specific car brand?

Solutions

1. You are a product manager for an e-commerce platform's mobile app. Recently, you've noticed a significant drop in the conversion rate for product listings. What steps would you take to address this issue and improve the conversion rate for the mobile app?

   The first step I'd take is to compare the observed drop in conversion rate with historical data to see if the drop is part of a trend that has happened in the past. I need to know whether this is a regularly occurring observation or if this is an anomaly that needs immediate attention.

   Next, I'd check against competitors or the industry to determine if this drop in conversion rate is an industry-specific problem or a company-specific problem. If this is a company-specific problem, then this would be particularly alarming.

   Afterwards, I would look at the metric by different segments, such as by geography, product category, or customer type. I want to see if there is a specific segment that is responsible for the majority of the issue.

   Once the primary segment or segments have been identified, I'd look into understanding what the root cause of the issue is. This could involve looking into changes in user behavior, mobile app updates, and mobile app usability issues.

   Once the root cause has been identified, the next step is to brainstorm solutions to address the decrease in conversion rate. This might include considering changes to product descriptions, pricing adjustments, optimizing app navigation, streamlining the checkout process, or resolving technical glitches.

   Finally, I would propose a plan that outlines specific actions that need to be taken to address the issue. This could involve conducting A/B testing to see if the proposed solution works, rolling out the changes to a subset of customers, and eventually rolling out changes to the entire customer base.

2. Imagine that you are the product manager for a recipe-sharing website. Recently, watch time for our cooking video tutorials has been lower than expected. You believe that viewers are increasingly preferring shorter-form content that is much more concise and engaging. All videos currently on the website are between 8-10 minutes.

   Design an A/B test to address this issue and test whether incorporating more shorter-form content would increase overall watch time.

   The objective is to increase overall watch time of cooking video tutorials on the website.

   The hypothesis is that by incorporating more shorter-form content that is concise and engaging, viewers will be more likely to watch the videos in their entirety, leading to an increase in overall watch time.

   The variable is video length. Let's define three different versions:

   - *Longer-length content (videos with a duration of 8-10 minutes)*
   - *Medium-length content (videos with a duration of 5-7 minutes)*
   - *Shorter-length content (videos with a duration of 2-4 minutes)*

   We can determine the minimum sample size needed using statistical tools by considering factors such as significance level, power, and expected effect size. This will ensure that the results of the A/B test are statistically significant.

   Next, we need to define three versions for a given recipe tutorial. Version A will remain exactly as it is now, with longer-length content. We will need to create a new Version B of that recipe tutorial that has medium-length content and a new Version C of that recipe tutorial that has shorter-length content.

We'll need to randomly assign visitors to either Version A, Version B, or Version C.

We'll also need to set up data tracking to monitor key user behavior metrics. We'll want to measure:

- *Click through rate on playing the video*
- *Average minutes of watch time for that recipe video*

The number of visitors times the click through rate times the average watch time gives us the total watch time for that recipe page. This is why these two metrics are selected.

After the testing period, we can analyze the collected data to see if the observed results for these two metrics are statistically significant.

Based on the results, we could run additional A/B tests to identify the optimal video length that will result in the most video watch time.

For example, if medium-length content performs best, we can test whether 5-minute, 6-minute, or 7-minute videos are optimal for maximizing video watch time.

3. You are the product manager at a subscription-based meditation app that offers a 3-day free trial followed by a monthly subscription. With a free trial, users can complete one meditation session per day. The company has observed a drop in conversion rates from the free trial to paid subscriptions. How would you go about optimizing the user flow to increase the conversion rate from trial users to paying subscribers?

The first step to optimize the user flow is to identify all of the steps:

- *User signs up for the 7-day free trial*
- *User looks through the app's offerings*

- *User picks their first meditation session (day 1)*
- *User completes their first meditation session (day 1)*
- *User picks their second meditation session (day 2)*
- *User completes their second meditation session (day 2)*
- *User picks their third meditation session (day 3)*
- *User completes their third meditation session (day 3)*
- *At the end of the trial period, the user is prompted to subscribe for full access*

Note that not every customer will follow this exact order. Some customers may do zero, one, or two meditation sessions before subscribing for full access. However, to be complete, we've outlined the full customer flow if a customer were to take full advantage of the free trial.

The assumption is that the more the customer uses the app, the more likely they will be to pay for it once the free trial ends.

The next step is to identify which steps are underperforming. Where do we see the steepest drop-off in conversion rates from one step to the next? Those should be the areas to prioritize.

Depending on which step has the steepest drop-off, we may want to propose one of the following solutions:

- *Incentivize early subscriptions: Offer a limited time discount or special offer to users who choose to subscribe before the end of the trial period*
- *Provide personalized meditation recommendations: Analyze user behavior and preferences during the trial to make it easier for users to select their next meditation session*

- *Enhance the onboarding experience: Provide guided onboarding tutorials or sessions to showcase the app's full capabilities and benefits, making it easier for the user to use for the first time*

- *Add more social proof and testimonials: Showcase success stories or positive reviews from existing subscribers to build trust and increase conversion rates*

- *Add interactive challenges and achievements: Gamify the app and encourage consistent engagement*

- *Add progress tracking and goal setting: Allow users to set meditation goals or intentions at the beginning of the trial period and provide tracking tools to hold them accountable*

- *Implement push notifications or in-app reminders: Prompt users to engage with the app throughout the day*

Once a potential solution has been identified, we can conduct an A/B test to see if the solution works. If it does, we can roll the feature out to the entire customer base and start testing additional potential solutions.

4. As a product manager for a music streaming service, you notice a decline in user retention rates. What steps would you take to investigate and address this issue?

   The first step I'd take is to compare the observed drop in retention rates with historical data to see if the drop is part of a trend that has happened in the past. I need to know whether this is a regularly occurring observation or if this is an anomaly that needs immediate attention.

   Next, I'd check against competitors or the industry to determine if this drop in retention rate is an industry-specific problem or a company-specific problem. If this is a company-specific problem, then this would be particularly alarming.

Afterwards, I would look at retention rates by different segments, such as by geography, customer type (e.g., free or paying user), or demographics (e.g., gender, age). I want to see if there is a specific segment that is responsible for the majority of the issue.

Once the primary segment or segments have been identified, I'd want to understand what the root cause of the issue is. This could involve looking into changes in user behavior, changes in our product offering, or changes happening in the market.

Once the root cause has been identified, the next step is to brainstorm solutions to address the decrease in retention rate. This might include considering changes to the user interface, library of available music, pricing model, integration and compatibility with other apps, or resolving technical glitches.

Finally, I would propose a plan that outlines specific actions that need to be taken to address the issue. This could involve conducting A/B testing to see if the proposed solution works, rolling out the changes to a subset of customers, and eventually rolling out changes to the entire customer base.

5. What are different ways of increasing checkout conversion? Propose a potential A/B test setup to assess the impact of each.

   There are many different ways to increase checkout conversion:

   - *Simplified checkout form*
     - *Control group: Existing checkout form with all required fields*
     - *Experimental group: Simplified checkout form with only essential fields, reducing the number of steps needed to complete the purchase*
   - *Progress indicators*

- *Control group: Checkout process without a progress indicator*
- *Experimental group: Introduce a visual progress indicator, showing users the steps involved in the checkout process*

- *Trust signals and security badges*
  - *Control group: Checkout page without trust signals or security badges*
  - *Experimental group: Add visible trust signals, such as SSL badges and security icons to enhance user trust*
- *Multiple payment options*
  - *Control group: Limited payment options*
  - *Experimental group: Introduce additional payment options, such as digital wallets, to cater to a broader range of user preferences*
- *Shipping cost transparency*
  - *Control group: Shipping costs revealed only at the end of the checkout process*
  - *Experimental group: Clearly communicate shipping costs upfront on the product page or in the cart to reduce unexpected surprises during checkout*
- *Social proof and reviews*
  - *Control group: Checkout page without social proof or customer reviews*

    - *Experimental group: Integrate customer reviews and testimonials on the checkout page to build trust and confidence in the purchase decision*

- *Popups for abandoned carts*

    - *Control group: No popups for abandoned carts*

    - *Experimental group: Implement popups with personalized offers or reminders for users with items in their carts who are about to leave the site*

- *Improved product page*

    - *Control group: Current version of the product page*

    - *Experimental group: Implement new images of the product and better product descriptions*

6. Identify the different steps a customer goes through when purchasing a new car. How could you improve each step to increase the likelihood that a customer purchases a specific car brand?

    There are six major steps in the car purchasing journey:

    Research and discovery:

    - *Utilize digital marketing and targeted advertising to reach potential buyers during their online research phase*

    - *Provide detailed specifications, features, and user reviews online to facilitate research*

    - *Create engaging video content showcasing the car's performance, safety features, and unique selling points*

    - *Implement a chatbot on the website to assist users with real-time inquiries during their research*

- *Foster a community around the specific car brand through social media and online forums*

Test drives:

- *Offer easily accessible test drive appointments with knowledgeable sales representatives*
- *Implement virtual or augmented reality experiences for remote test drives*
- *Provide incentives, such as exclusive test drive events or extended test drive periods*

Financing and price negotiation:

- *Offer transparent pricing information online to build trust*
- *Provide financing calculators and options for pre-approval to streamline the process*
- *Consider offering loyalty programs or exclusive discounts for specific financing options*

Purchase agreement and documentation:

- *Streamline the paperwork process with digital documentation and e-signature options*
- *Provide clear explanations of terms, fees, and warranties*
- *Offer online tools for customers to review and sign documents at their convenience*

Delivery and vehicle handover:

- *Include a personalized vehicle walkthrough*

- *Provide comprehensive tutorials on the car's features and technology*
- *Create a memorable delivery event, such as a photo opportunity or special gift for the new car owner*

Post-purchase follow-up:

- *Offer ongoing communication about maintenance schedules, service reminders, and updates*
- *Create loyalty programs that reward customers for repeat purchases or referrals*
- *Encourage satisfied customers to share their experiences through testimonials and reviews*

To prioritize which actions to take, we would want to determine which step of the purchase process is performing the most poorly.

Ideally, we would want to benchmark our company's performance in each step with industry benchmarks or with our major competitors.

12. Technical Questions

What are technical questions?

Technical questions assess your understanding of technical concepts relevant to the product that you'd be managing.

Product managers do not necessarily need to have the same level of technical expertise as engineers, but they do need to have a grasp of technical concepts to effectively communicate and collaborate with development teams.

Examples of technical questions include:

- What is an API?
- What are a few different algorithms to sort elements?
- What are the different components of a database?
- What are the different components you need to have a website running?

What are interviewers looking for?

There are three major skills and qualities that interviewers look for when asking technical questions:

- **Technical knowledge**: Familiarity with the technical concepts related to the product
- **Domain knowledge**: Industry-specific knowledge that is relevant to the product
- **Ability to communicate technical concepts**: Ability to communicate technical information to non-technical stakeholders

What technical concepts do I need to know?

There is an extremely wide range of potential technical concepts you could be asked depending on the industry, company, and team you are interviewing for.

It is not possible to cover every single potential technical concept you could be asked. However, there are a few common technical concepts that are fundamental to being a PM that you should be familiar with:

- Basic programming concepts
- Basic algorithms
- Web technologies
- Database fundamentals
- APIs
- System architecture and design

- Agile/scrum methodologies

We'll provide a brief overview of all of these major technical concepts. However, when interviewing, make sure to understand which technical concepts are most relevant to the role and focus more of your time preparing for those technical questions.

Basic programming concepts

1. Variables

A variable is a container that holds data that can be changed during program execution. It has a name and a value.

Example:

- *name = "John"*
- *age = 30*

2. Data types

Data types define the type of data that a variable can hold. Common data types include:

- **Integers**: A number with no decimal or fractional part
- **Floating-point numbers**: Decimals
- **Strings**: Text
- **Booleans**: True or false
- **Arrays and lists**: A collection of values stored under a single variable name
- **Hash tables**: Maps keys to values for efficient data retrieval

- **Trees**: Hierarchical data structure with a root node at the top and branches extending downwards

- **Graphs**: Consists of a set of nodes, also known as vertices, connected by edges. These connects can be directed (one-way) or undirected (two-way)

3. Operators

Operators are symbols or keywords that represent a specific mathematical or logical action or process.

Examples of operators include:

- **Arithmetic operators**: addition, subtraction, multiplication, and division

- **Logical operators**: and, or, not

- **Comparison operators**: equal to, not equal to, greater than, less than, greater than or equal to, less than or equal to

4. Conditional statements

Conditional statements allow different code blocks to be executed based on certain conditions.

Examples of conditional statements include:

- If

- Else if

- Else

5. Loops

Loops allow a block of code to be executed repeatedly.

Examples of loops include:

- For loop: executes a block of code a specific number of times
- While loop: repeatedly executes a block of code as long as a specified condition is true

6. Functions

Functions are blocks of code that perform a specific task. They can be called and can return a value.

Examples:

- *Function that adds two numbers and returns the result*
- *Function that calculates the factorial of a number*
- *Function that prints a greeting*

7. Objects and classes

A class is a blueprint or template for creating objects. It specifies what attributes (data) and methods (functions) an object of that class will have.

An object is an instance of a class. It is a specific entity created based on the blueprint or template provided by a class.

Example: *A "Car" class defines the make, model, and year of a car. An object of that class would be a specific car with its unique properties.*

8. Pointers

A pointer is a variable that holds the memory address of another variable. It "points" to the location in memory where a value is stored.

Example: *You can have a variable 'x' that holds a value. You can have a pointer that contains the memory address of 'x.' By using the pointer, you can access and modify the value of 'x' without directly referencing it.*

9. Recursion

Recursion is a technique in which a function calls itself to solve a problem.

A recursive function typically has two parts: a base case and a recursive case. The base case serves as the exit condition, stopping the recursive calls, while the recursive case involves the function calling itself with a modified input, moving towards the base case.

Example: *The factorial of a non-negative integer 'n', denoted as 'n!', is the product of all positive integers less than or equal to 'n'. We can define n! = n * (n-1)! to solve for 5!*

- *5! = 5 * 4!*
- *4! = 4 * 3!*
- *3! = 3 * 2!*
- *2! = 2 * 1!*
- *1! = 1 (base case)*
- *Therefore, 5! = 5 * 4 * 3 * 2 * 1 = 120*

Basic Algorithms

An algorithm is a well-defined set of instructions or rules that specify a sequence of operations to be performed in a finite amount of time to accomplish a specific task or solve a particular problem.

Having a basic understanding of common algorithms can be beneficial for understanding code efficiency and making informed decisions in product development.

Below are some common algorithms you should be familiar with:

1. **Sorting algorithms**

   Bubble sort: Compares adjacent elements and swaps them if they are in the wrong order. It repeatedly passes through the list until it's sorted.

   Selection sort: Divides the input list into a sorted and an unsorted region. It repeatedly selects either the smallest or largest element from the unsorted region and moves it to the sorted region.

   Insertion sort: Builds the final sorted array one element at a time. It takes an element from the unsorted part and inserts it into the correct position in the sorted part.

2. **Searching algorithms**

   Binary search: Assumes the list is sorted and repeatedly divides the search space in half until the target element is found or determines that the element is not present.

   Linear search: Goes through each element in the list one by one until it finds the target element or reaches the end.

3. **Graph algorithms**

   Depth-First Search (DFS): Explores as far as possible along each branch before backtracking.

   Breadth-First Search (BFS): Explores all the vertices at the current depth prior to moving on to vertices at the next depth level.

4. **Two-Pointers Technique**

   Involves using two pointers to traverse a data structure. It's often used for problems that involve finding a pair or a subarray that meets certain conditions.

5. **Sliding Window Technique**

Maintains a subset of elements within a fixed-size window that slides over the data. It is useful for problems involving sequence or subarray operations.

Big O Notation

In addition to these algorithms, you should be familiar with Big O Notation, which is used to compare the complexity of different algorithms.

Big O Notation provides the upper bound on the time or space complexity of an algorithm in the worst-case scenario. It helps understand how the runtime or memory requirements of an algorithm scale with the size of the input.

***Example**: An algorithm with a time complexity of O(n) means that the runtime of the algorithm grows linearly with the size of the input. An algorithm with $O(n^2)$ means that the runtime grows quadratically with the size of the input.*

Web technologies

Web technologies form the foundation of the internet and are crucial for building and managing websites and web applications.

Below is an overview of the key components of web technologies:

1. HTML

HTML stands for Hypertext Markup Language. It provides the basic structure and content of a webpage using elements and tags.

Examples:

- *<title>*
- *<body>*
- *<p>*

2. CSS

CSS stands for Cascading Style Sheets. It controls aspects such as colors, fonts, spacing, and positioning.

Examples:

- *Font-family: Arial, sans-serif*
- *color: blue*
- *background-color: #f0f0f0*

3. JavaScript

JavaScript is a programming language that enables interactivity and dynamic behavior on web pages. It is executed in the browser.

4. Front-End Frameworks and Libraries

Front-end frameworks such as React, Angular, and Vue.js provide pre-built components and structures to streamline web development.

5. Server-Side Technologies

Server-side technologies handle operations on the server. This includes programming languages such as JavaScript, Python, Ruby, Java, and PHP.

6. Databases and Database Management

Databases store, retrieve, and manage data. There are different types, including relational databases and NoSQL databases. We'll cover databases in more detail in the next section.

7. Web Hosting and Development

Web applications are hosted on servers. Services like AWS, Google Cloud, and Heroku provide platforms for hosting and deploying web applications.

8. HTTP and HTTPS

HTTP stands for Hypertext Transfer Protocol. It is the protocol used for transmitting data over the internet. HTTPS is a secure version.

Database fundamentals

Databases play a crucial role in data organization, storage, and computing. They are a fundamental component of many software applications and play a critical role in managing and manipulating data efficiently.

Below is an overview of what you should know about databases.

What is a database?

A database is an organized collection of structured information or data, typically stored electronically in a computer system. Databases make it easy to store, retrieve, modify, and manage information.

Example: *In a database of customers, data can be organized into tables, which consists of rows and columns. Each row represents a customer. Each column represents a specific attribute or piece of information related to the customer, such as the customer's name, address, phone number, and email.*

Databases are used in a wide range of applications, ranging from simple ones like address books or inventory management systems to large-scale enterprise systems, social media platforms, and more.

What are the different types of databases?

There are several types of databases, each designed to handle specific types of data and applications. The most common types of databases include:

- **Relational database**: Organizes data into tables with rows and columns
- **NoSQL database**: Provides a flexible data model that is designed to handle large volumes of unstructured or semi-structured data. It does not adhere to the traditional row and column structure of a relational database. Types of NoSQL databases include:
    - **Document-oriented**: Stores data in semi-structured documents
    - **Key-value stores**: Stores data in key-value pairs
    - **Column-family stores**: Organizes data into columns rather than rows
    - **Graph databases**: Organizes data in terms of nodes and edges, which represent entities and the relationships between them. These are used for highly connected data
- **Object-oriented database**: Stores data in objects. Used to work with object-oriented programming languages
- **Hierarchical database**: Organizes data in a tree-like structure with parent-child relationships, where each record in the database has one parent, but can have multiple children
- **Network database**: Extends the hierarchical database model by allowing many-to-many relationships between records. A child record can have multiple parents.

What are the different components of a database?

There are five main components of a database: hardware, software, data, procedure, and database access language.

- **Hardware**: The physical devices that make up the computer system on which the database is hosted. This includes components such as servers, storage devices, and networking equipment

- **Software**: A set of programs used to manage the database, consisting of the database management system (DBMS), the operating system, the network software for sharing the data, and the applications that access the data

- **Data**: The information that is stored in the database. It can be in a variety of formats, such as text, images, or video

- **Procedure**: The instructions or set of operations that define how the database system should operate. Procedures include guidelines for backups, recovery, data validation, and other maintenance tasks

- **Database access language**: The languages and interfaces used to create, access, and modify data. The most common language used for this is SQL (Structured Query Language)

APIs

What is an API?

An API, or Application Programming Interface, is a set of rules and protocols that allows different software applications to communicate with each other. It defines the methods and data formats that applications can use to request and exchange information.

APIs serve various purposes and play a crucial role in modern software development. Key uses include:

- Integrating various services and functionalities, allowing them to work together seamlessly

- Providing a standardized way for developers to access external services, such as social media platforms, payment gateways, and mapping services

- Allowing applications to retrieve and manipulate data from databases, both locally and over the internet

- Facilitating automation by allowing different software components to interact programmatically

- Facilitating third-party developers to create applications or plugins that extend the functionality of their platforms

- Managing user authentication and authorization

There are APIs that allow applications to interact with hardware, operating systems, databases, and cloud services to name a few.

What are the different types of APIs?

There are several different types of APIs you should be familiar with:

- **Open APIs**: Also known as public APIs, are publicly available for developers and other users with minimal restrictions. They can be freely accessed and used by anyone

- **Internal APIs**: Also known as private APIs, are intended for use within a specific organization or company. They are not meant for external developers

- **Partner APIs**: Designed for use by specific partners or third-party companies, often through a formal agreement

- **Composite APIs**: Allow developers to access multiple endpoints or services in a single request. They are useful for reducing the number of API calls needed to accomplish a task

- **RESTful APIs**: Stands for Representational State Transfer APIs, a type of web API that follows a set of architectural principles making them stateless, cacheable, and utilizing standard HTTP methods. These are commonly used for web services

- **SOAP APIs**: Stands for Simple Object Access Protocol APIs, which use XML-based messaging protocols for exchanging information over a network. They are more rigid and have more structure compared to RESTful APIs

- **GraphQL APIs**: A query language for APIs that allows clients to request exactly the data they need. It provides a more flexible and efficient approach compared to traditional RESTful APIs, especially for complex and diverse data requirements

- **WebSocket APIs**: Allow for real-time, bidirectional communication between a client and a server. This enables applications to establish a continuous connection for instant updates and data exchanges

- **Library or Framework APIs**: Pre-defined functions and routines that developers can use to simplify complex tasks or interact with specific programming libraries or frameworks

How does an API work?

Below are the major steps of how an API works:

Request

The process begins with a client application, such as a web browser or mobile app, initiating a request. The request is made to access a service or resource provided by another software component or system.

Specifically, the client sends an HTTP request to a specific URL, known as an API endpoint. An API endpoint represents a specific resource or action that the API can perform.

The client uses one of the standard HTTP methods to indicate the type of action it wants to perform on the endpoint.

Along with the request, the client may send additional information in the form of headers, metadata about the request, and parameters, additional context or instructions to the API.

Authentication

APIs have different authentication mechanisms, such as API keys or OAuth tokens. This ensures that only authorized users or applications can access the API.

Processing

The API server receives the request and processes it based on the provided endpoint, method, headers, and parameters.

This may involve tasks such as querying a database, performing calculations, or interacting with other services.

Response

After processing the request, the API server generates a response. The response typically includes an HTTP status code that indicates the success or failure of the request and a body containing the data information requested by the client.

The data in the response body is usually formatted in a standard way, such as JSON or XML. These formats provide a structured way to easily parse the data.

The response is sent back to the client over the network, using the HTTP protocol.

Client Handling

Once the client application receives a response, it will process it based on the information provided.

This could involve any action such as displaying data to a user or further processing the information.

System architecture and design

What is system architecture and design?

System architecture and design is the process of planning and defining the structure, components, and behavior of a software system or application.

It involves making high-level decisions about how the system will be organized and how its various parts will interact with each other to achieve specific goals.

What are key considerations in system architecture and design?

There are several considerations that should be made when defining a system architecture or design.

- **Functional requirements**: Understanding the purpose of the system, the tasks it needs to perform, and the features it should provide

- **Component identification**: Identifying the major components of the system and how they will interact with each other

- **Data management**: Deciding how data will be stored, retrieved, and manipulated within the system

- **User interface design**: Determining how users will interact with the system

- **Technology stack**: Choosing the appropriate programming languages, frameworks, libraries, and tools for building the system
- **Security measures**: Planning for security features such as authentication, authorization, encryption, and protection against common security threats
- **Scalability measures**: Designing the system to handle expected loads and increased usage
- **Availability measures**: Planning for how the system can be operational and accessible to users when needed without interruption
- **Maintainability measures**: Planning for how the system can be maintained, updated, and modified over time
- **Error handling and recovery**: Defining strategies for handling errors, logging, and implementing mechanisms for system recovery
- **Testing and quality assurance**: Developing a test strategy to ensure that the system functions correctly and meets all requirements

Agile/scrum methodologies

Agile and scrum are popular methodologies used in software development to manage projects and deliver products in an iterative and flexible manner.

As a product manager, you should be familiar with these methodologies as you will likely be using them on the job.

Below is a basic primer of these methodologies:

Agile methodology

Agile is an iterative and flexible approach to software development that emphasizes collaboration, customer feedback, and incremental progress.

The agile methodology allows teams to respond quickly to changing requirements and deliver value to customers in shorter timeframes.

Key agile principles include:

- Delivering working software to customers in small, incremental releases, with a preference for shorter timeframes

- Encouraging adaptability to changing requirements, even late in the development process

- Defining progress as working software rather than documentation

- Setting up regular collaboration between customers, stakeholders, and the development team to ensure that the product meets business goals and user needs

- Trusting individuals to do their best work and providing them with the support they need

- Focusing on simplicity and avoiding unnecessary complexity

- Encouraging self-organizing teams, which are believed to make the best decisions regarding design and implementation

Agile projects are divided into small increments, called "iterations" or "sprints." Each increment typically lasts between 2-4 weeks.

Agile teams are typically small, cross-functional groups that include developers, testers, designers, and other necessary roles.

The major challenges to Agile practices is that it requires discipline to follow and that some teams may find it challenging to adapt to rapidly changing requirements.

Scrum framework

Scrum is a specific Agile framework that provides a structured way to implement Agile principles. It defines the roles, events, and artifacts to facilitate effective collaboration and delivery of product.

Scrum has three roles: product owner, scrum master, and the development team members.

- **Product owner**: Responsible for ensuring that the team is aligned with the overall product goals by defining and prioritizing product features and tasks

- **Scrum master**: Responsible for ensuring that the team is operating as efficiently as possible. The Scrum master keeps the team on track, plans and leads meetings, and removes obstacles the team may face

- **Development team members**: Responsible for delivering the product increment

Scrum defines several events, sometimes called ceremonies, that occur inside each sprint:

- **Sprint planning**: Meeting at the beginning of each sprint to plan the work for the upcoming iteration

- **Sprint review**: Meeting at the end of the sprint to review and demonstrate the completed work to stakeholders.

- **Sprint retrospective**: Meeting at the end of the sprint for the team to reflect on their process and identify improvements

- **Daily scrum**: Brief daily meeting for the development team to synchronize and plan their work

Scrum artifacts are items that provide information about the project's process, work to be done, or the product itself.

- **Product backlog**: An ordered list of all the features, enhancements, bug fixes, and other work that needs to be done on the product. It represents the requirements and priorities set by the product owner

- **Sprint backlog**: A subset of the product backlog that contains the work selected by the development team to be completed during a specific sprint

- **Increment**: The sum of all the completed product backlog items at the end of a sprint. It represents all of the product progress that is in a usable and functional state.

Teams may tailor these practices to best suit their specific needs.

It is more important to focus on Agile principles and adapt the methodology or framework to fit the team's unique circumstances than to follow a specific framework exactly.

Summary

- Technical questions assess your understanding of technical concepts relevant to the product you'd be managing
- Common technical concepts that are fundamental to being a PM that you should be familiar with include:
    - Basic programming concepts
    - Basic algorithms
    - Web technologies
    - Database fundamentals
    - APIs
    - System architecture and design
    - Agile / scrum methodologies

Practice

1. Explain the difference between a "for loop" and a "while loop."

2. What is the Big O Notation of the following algorithms?

    - Accessing an element in an array by its index
    - Finding the maximum element in an unsorted list
    - An algorithm with two nested loops

3. Explain what recursion is.

4. What is the difference between HTML, CSS, and JavaScript?

5. What is the difference between a relational database and a NoSQL database?

6. How does an API work?

7. What are some key considerations in system architecture and design?

8. What are the major agile methodology principles?

Solutions

1. Explain the difference between a "for loop" and a "while loop."

   A "for loop" is used when we know in advance the number of times a certain block of code needs to be executed. It's especially useful for iterating over a sequence of elements, such as a list or a range of numbers.

   A "while loop" is used when we need to repeat a block of code as long as a certain condition holds true. It is useful in scenarios where the number of iterations is not known beforehand and depends on a specific condition. It requires careful handling to avoid infinite loops, where the condition never becomes false.

2. What is the Big O Notation of the following algorithms?

   - Accessing an element in an array by its index

     This algorithm's runtime does not depend on the size of the input. It performs a constant amount of work regardless of how large the input is. Therefore, the Big O Notation is: O(1).

   - Finding the maximum element in an unsorted list

     The runtime of this algorithm grows linearly with the size of the input. The Big O Notation is: O(n).

   - An algorithm with two nested loops

     This algorithm's runtime is proportional to the square of the input size since it involves two nested loops. Therefore, the Big O Notation is: $O(n^2)$.

3. Explain what recursion is.

Recursion is when a function calls itself in its own definition. In simpler terms, it's a process where a function solves a problem by breaking it down into smaller instances of the same problem.

A recursive function typically has two parts: a base case and a recursive case. The base case serves as the exit condition, stopping the recursive calls, while the recursive case involves the function calling itself with a modified input, moving towards the base case.

4. What is the difference between HTML, CSS, and JavaScript?

HTML is the standard markup language for creating the structure of a web page. It defines the elements and tags that structure the content on a webpage, such as headings, paragraphs, lists, links, images, and more.

CSS is a styling language that complements HTML by describing how the elements on a webpage should be visually presented. It controls the layout, colors, fonts, spacing, and overall visual styling of HTML elements.

JavaScript is a programming language that enables dynamic, interactive behavior on a webpage. It allows developers to manipulate the content and behavior of a webpage in response to user interactions. JavaScript can be used to create features like form validation, animations, updating content dynamically, and communicating with servers.

5. What is the difference between a relational database and a NoSQL database?

Relational databases follow a structured model in which data is organized into tables with rows and columns. They have a predefined schema that defines the structure of the data, including the data types and relationships. Relational databases are well-suited for applications with complex queries and transactions in which data integrity and consistency are crucial.

NoSQL databases are designed to handle unstructured or semi-structured data. They support a variety of data models, including document-oriented, key-value, column-family, and graph formats. NoSQL databases are schema-less or have a dynamic schema, allowing for flexible data storage without a predefined structure. They are suitable for scenarios where data is evolving rapidly and the schema is not well-defined in advance.

6. How does an API work?

An API, or Application Programming Interface, acts as a bridge that allows different software applications to communicate and interact with each other. It defines a set of rules and protocols for building and interacting with software components.

Here's a high-level overview of how an API works:

- *Request: An API is typically initiated when one software component, known as the client, sends a request to another component, known as the server*

- *Authentication: APIs have different authentication mechanisms, such as API keys or OAuth tokens. This ensures that only authorized users or applications can access the API*

- *Processing: Upon receiving the request, the server processes it according to the rules defined by the API. This might involve querying a database or performing calculations*

- *Response: After processing the request, the server sends back a response to the client. This response contains the requested data or the result of the operation. The response is typically formatted in a standard data interchange format, such as JSON or XML, making it easy for the client to interpret*

- *Client Handling: Once the client application receives a response, it will process it based on the information provided*

7. What are some key considerations in system architecture and design?

   Key considerations in system architecture and design include the following:

   - ***Functional requirements**: Understanding the purpose of the system, the tasks it needs to perform, and the features it should provide*

   - ***Component identification**: Identifying the major components of the system and how they will interact with each other*

   - ***Data management**: Deciding how data will be stored, retrieved, and manipulated within the system*

   - ***User interface design**: Determining how users will interact with the system*

   - ***Technology stack**: Choosing the appropriate programming languages, frameworks, libraries, and tools for building the system*

   - ***Security measures**: Planning for security features such as authentication, authorization, encryption, and protection against common security threats*

   - ***Scalability measures**: Designing the system to handle expected loads and increased usage*

   - ***Availability measures**: Planning for how the system can be operational and accessible to users when needed without interruption*

   - ***Maintainability measures**: Planning for how the system can be maintained, updated, and modified over time*

- ***Error handling and recovery***: *Defining strategies for handling errors, logging, and implementing mechanisms for system recovery*

- ***Testing and quality assurance***: *Developing a test strategy to ensure that the system functions correctly and meets all requirements*

8. What are the major agile methodology principles?

   Major agile methodology principles include the following:

   - *Delivering working software frequently*
   - *Welcoming changing requirements, even late in the process*
   - *Collaborating closely with the customer*
   - *Encouraging self-organizing teams*
   - *Encouraging simplicity in both the design and implementation of the software*

Bonus Tip: To test yourself to see if you truly understand a technical concept, try to explain it to a fifth grader. The simpler you can explain or teach a concept, the better you understand it.

13. Take-Home Assignments

What are take-home assignments?

Take-home assignments are tasks or projects that candidates are asked to complete on their own time and submit as part of the interview process.

For take-home assignments, you'll be asked to prepare a few slides answering a specific prompt. You may also be asked to present these slides in front of an interviewer who will discuss your work and ask follow-up questions.

These take-home assignments are usually given sometime in the early and middle interview rounds. They may or may not have a time limit for completion.

These assignments are designed to assess a candidate's skills, knowledge, and approach to real-world product manager scenarios or situations.

Here are a few examples of common take-home assignments:

- **Product design or improvement**: You are asked to design or improve a particular product

- **Product roadmap planning**: You are asked to create a product roadmap for a given scenario, outlining key features, milestones, and release schedule

- **Product prioritization**: You are given a list of potential features or initiatives for a product and asked to prioritize them based on a set of criteria

- **Product analysis**: You are asked to analyze an existing product's strengths and weaknesses and provide recommendations for improvement

- **Product metrics and KPIs**: You are given a set of metrics or KPIs and asked to explain how you would use them to measure the success of a product

- **Technical feasibility assessment**: You are asked to assess the technical feasibility of a proposed feature or product. This is only asked for PM roles that require technical knowledge

- **User experience design**: You are given a user problem and asked to design a user interface or flow for a specific feature or product

Take-home assignments allow you to showcase your knowledge and skills, but they also give you insight into the type of work you might be doing if you join the company.

What are interviewers looking for?

There are a number of skills and qualities interviewers look for when giving take-home assignments:

- **Product understanding**: Interviewers want to see how you approach product management, from ideation to development, launch, and iteration

- **Strategic thinking**: Interviewers want to assess your ability to think strategically about product development, market positioning, and long-term business goals

- **Creativity and innovation**: Interviewers want to see your ability to think outside the box and develop innovative solutions to problems

- **Technical proficiency**: For technical product manager roles, interviewers want to assess your technical understanding and aptitude

- **Communication skills**: Interviewers want to see how effectively you can articulate your ideas, plans, and strategies

While there are a lot of skills and qualities being assessed, the good news is that take home assignments are often untimed.

Some candidates may spend only a few hours working on the take-home assignment, while others may spend multiple days or even a week working on them.

The more time you invest in the take-home assignment, the better you'll be able to demonstrate your knowledge and skills.

How to complete take-home assignments

Completing a take-home assignment for PM interviews requires careful planning, research, analysis, and effective communication. Follow these seven steps to submit the highest quality work.

1. Read the instructions carefully

Start by thoroughly reading the instructions of the take-home assignment provided to you. The easiest way to fail a take-home assignment is to submit the wrong assignment.

- What is the objective of the assignment?
- In what type of format should the assignment be submitted?
- What are all components that should be included in the submission?
- When is the take-home assignment due?

2. Ask clarifying questions

Most of the time, the instructions for the take-home assignment should be comprehensive and clear.

However, if you have any important questions or clarifications on the assignment, don't hesitate to reach out to the recruiter or interviewer.

It is better to seek clarification and confirmation early on rather than wasting hours making the wrong assumptions.

3. Research and gather information

Before starting the assignment, it is important to ensure that you have all the information you need to complete it.

Depending on what the prompt is for your take-home assignment, you may need to conduct research or gather further information. This may entail conducting market research, analyzing competitors, or researching the company.

4. Create an outline

When you have finished researching and gathering all of the information that you need, create an outline.

An outline will help you organize your thoughts in a clear, structured way. This will help you work more efficiently as you complete the assignment.

- What is your ultimate answer or recommendation to the take-home assignment?
- How many slides do you need to create?
- What is going to be on each slide?
- How are you going to display the content on each slide?
- In what order should the slides go?

5. Create your slides

The goal of making presentation slides is to make your work and your ultimate answer or recommendation shine. You can do amazing research, analysis, and have an outstanding recommendation or answer, but the interviewer won't be able to see this if you can't make great slides.

Your slides need to tell a compelling story that is clear, easy to follow, and well supported by evidence.

You can use the following structure when making your presentation slides:

- Title
- Executive summary
- Supporting analysis slides

- Recommendation / summary
- Risks & mitigations
- Next steps
- Appendix

We'll go through each section to specify what you should include. However, you'll likely need to pick and choose which slides to include or exclude depending on the context of the assignment and the slide limit.

For example, if you are given a very small slide limit, you may want to combine the risks & mitigations and next steps slide or even exclude an executive summary.

Title: Your title slide should be simple. Include a title for your presentation and your name. If you'd like, you can also include a logo of the company you are interviewing with.

Executive summary: This slide consists entirely of bullet points that summarize your answer and the supporting evidence.

If a person were just to read the executive summary, they should be able to understand the main points of the entire presentation.

Executive summaries tend to be too long and wordy. Therefore, make every effort to make your bullets as concise as possible. Only include the most important key takeaways.

Supporting analysis slides: These slides will be the bulk of your presentation. In this section, you will include diagrams, mockups, charts, graphs, tables, or bullet points that support your answer or recommendation.

Recommendation / summary: This slide should show your final recommendation or summary of the answer. It should cover your recommendation in more detail than the executive summary.

You may think that it is redundant to summarize the answer or recommendation twice, once in the executive summary and once on this slide, but a great presentation that is easy to understand follows this pattern:

- Informs the audience what you are going to tell them
- Gives the audience the information
- Reminds the audience what you have just told them

Risks & mitigations: Include a slide that lists the major risks of your recommendation. This demonstrates to the interviewer that you have thoroughly thought through all of the potential implications.

After each risk, list what actions could be taken to mitigate these risks. If you provide a reasonable plan for managing the potential risks, your answer or recommendation will be much stronger.

If the data challenge has a slide limit, you can leave out this section and put it in the appendix instead.

Next steps: Include a few bullet points outlining potential next steps you would take if you had more data or more time. This demonstrates initiative and ownership.

Ask yourself the following questions:

- What other open questions do you have?
- What else would you need to know to feel more confident in your answer or recommendation?
- What could you do to find answers to these questions?
- How would you test or implement your answer or recommendation?

Appendix: You can include backup slides in the appendix, which typically does not count towards the slide limit. These are slides that were not important enough to make it into the main presentation.

Backup slides can also be slides that show assumptions, backup calculations, or additional diagrams and mockups to your main supporting analysis slides. Including these slides shows your work to the interviewer and demonstrates attention to detail.

Additional tips: Here are a few best practices to follow when creating your slides:

- Write descriptive slide titles that clearly communicate the main message; the interviewer should know what the slide is going to show just by reading the title

- All of the titles of your slides should collectively read like a story; the interviewer should be able to understand the main points of your presentation just by reading the titles

- Avoid overcrowding your slides by having only one key message on each slide

- Use a variety of different slide formats, such as bullets, charts, graphs, tables, diagrams, and mockups

- Use bolding, circles, boxes, color, or call-out boxes to call attention to the most important messages on each slide

6. Proofread and review

After making your slides, take a short break and then review all of your slides thoroughly from beginning to end.

Focus on improving any of the following:

- Are there are any errors or typos that need to be fixed?

- Are the slides easy to understand?

- Do the slides tell the complete story of your answer or recommendation?
- Are the slides interesting and eye-catching?

7. Prepare for the presentation

Once you have finished reviewing and putting the final touches on your slides, it is time to prepare for the presentation.

To make your presentation go more smoothly, you should practice your presentation a few times in front of a mirror or in front of a friend or partner who can provide you with feedback.

Also, try to anticipate what potential questions your interviewer may ask you. Prepare answers to each of these potential questions.

Take-home assignment example

Example: *Prepare a presentation that proposes how you would improve Venmo, an app that allows users to pay and request money from friends and family. Keep your presentation to a maximum of eight slides.*

1. The title slide is simple, showing an informative title of the presentation and the author.

Three Ways to Improve Venmo for Family & Social Groups

Taylor Warfield

2. The executive summary provides a concise overview of the entire presentation. After reading it, the audience will know exactly what to expect.

Executive summary

- We considered three major customer segments and ultimately decided to focus on **family & social groups** because we believe they account for the majority of users
- We decided to focus on three pain points: **difficulty splitting bills fairly**, **notification fatigue**, and **recurring payments**
- To address splitting bills fairly, we propose **adding additional split options** (e.g., by percentage, by dollar amount, by shares, by manual adjustments)
- To address notification fatigue, we propose **batching notifications** into a single summary per day, week, or month
- To address recurring payments, we propose **adding scheduled recurring payments or requests** to save users time and prevent them from forgetting
- Potential risks of rolling out these new product features include: decreased user engagement, poor customer experience, and technical issues; designing and launching A/B tests will help assess these risks before full rollout

3. This slide shows how we considered different customer segments and selected one to focus on to narrow the scope of the assignment.

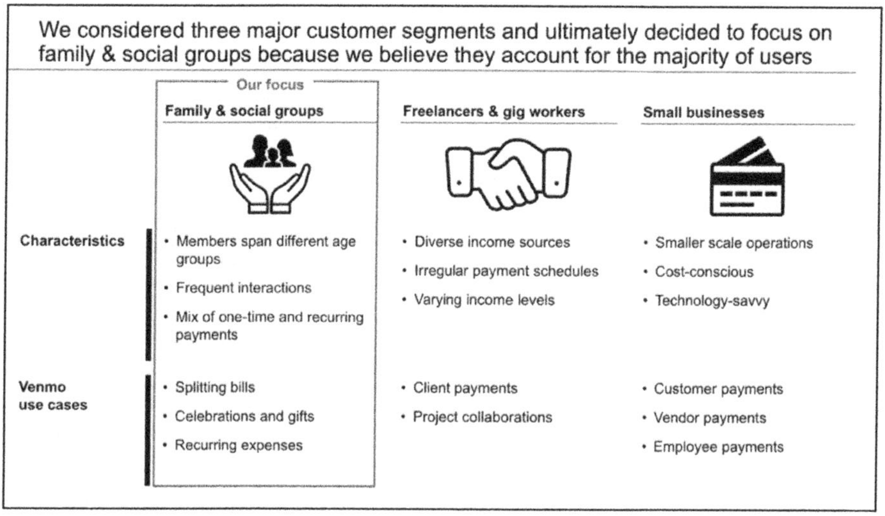

4. This slide shows how we considered multiple pain points and selected a few to focus on, further narrowing the scope of the assignment and making it more manageable.

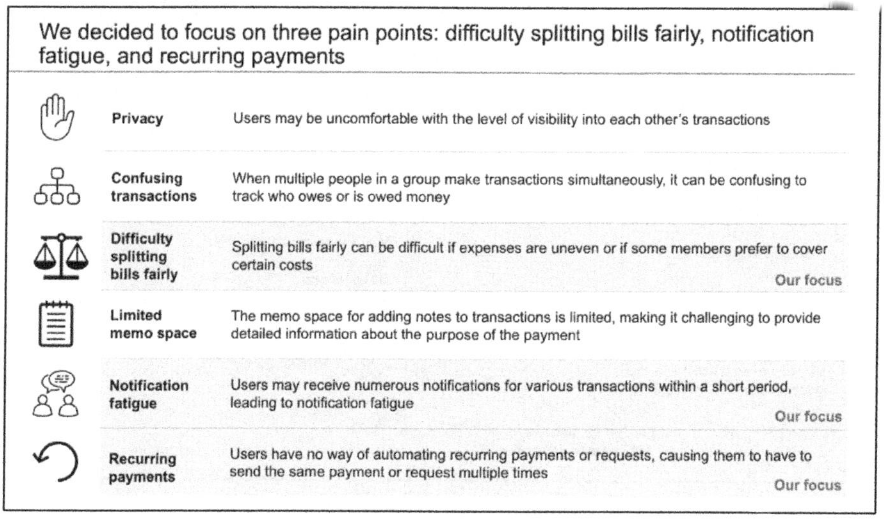

5. This slide gives the first recommendation of how we would improve the product.

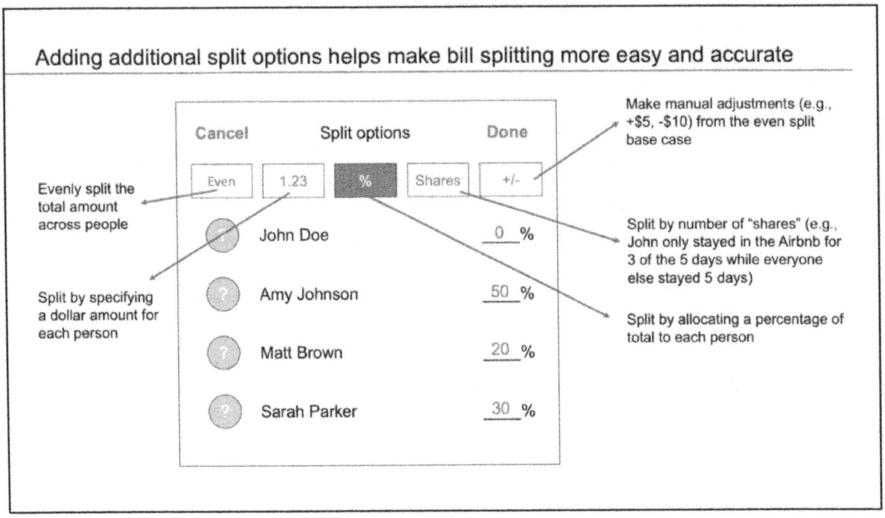

6. This slide gives the second recommendation of how we would improve the product.

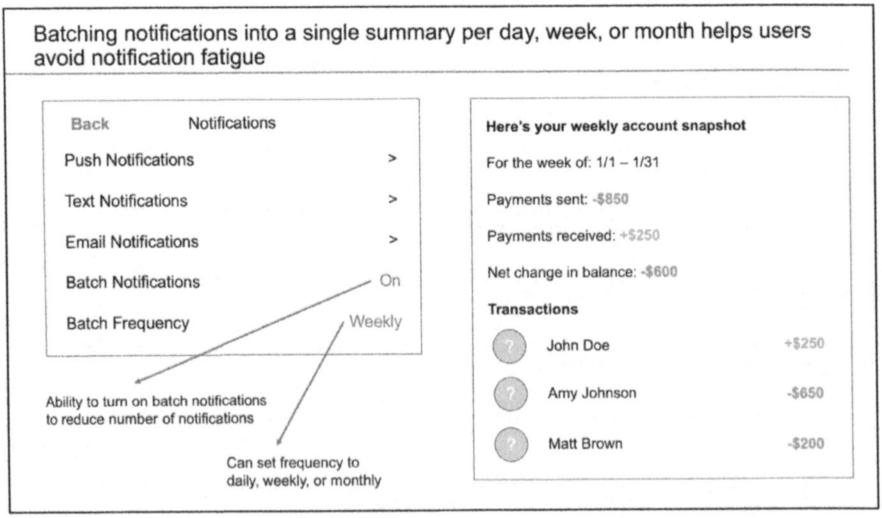

7. This slide gives the third recommendation of how we would improve the product.

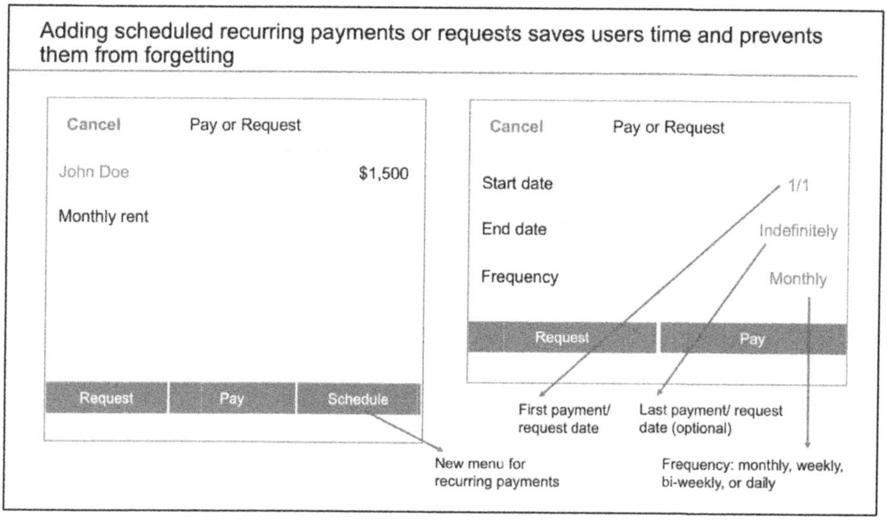

8. This slide combines risks and next steps. We want to demonstrate that we can think critically about the possible implications of our recommendations. We also want to demonstrate that we proactively think about what the next steps should be.

There are several risks for each proposed product feature; A/B tests will enable assessment of these risks before feature is rolled out to all customers

Risks

- Adding additional split options
  - May add too much complexity to the user interface, potentially confusing users
  - More splitting options increases the likelihood of user error, leading to increased inaccuracies
- Batching notifications
  - May lead to reduced user engagement
  - May lead to poor customer experience if notifications are too delayed
- Adding scheduled recurring payments or requests
  - Scheduled recurring payments may encounter technical issues (e.g., if a user's balance is insufficient)
  - Security and safety concerns of scheduling recurring payments indefinitely or for long periods of time

Next steps

- Design A/B test for each proposed product feature
- Launch A/B test for a subset of users
- Analyze A/B test results
- Decide on if further product feature modifications are needed or if ready to roll out to all users

Summary

- Take-home assignments ask you to prepare a few slides answering a specific prompt; you may also be asked to present these slides in front of an interviewer
- How to complete take-home assignments
  - Read the instructions carefully
  - Ask clarifying questions
  - Research and gather information
  - Create an outline
  - Create your slides
  - Proofread and review
  - Prepare for the presentation
- You can use the following structure when making your presentation slides
  - Title
  - Executive summary
  - Supporting analysis slides
  - Recommendation / summary
  - Risks & mitigations
  - Next steps
  - Appendix

- Follow these best practices when creating slides to make your presentation clear and easy to understand
    - Write descriptive slide titles that communicate the main message of the slide
    - All of the titles of your slides should collectively read like a story
    - Avoid overcrowding your slides by having only one key message for each slide
    - Use a variety of slide formats, such as bullets, charts, graphs, tables, diagrams, and mockups
    - Use bolding, circles, boxes, color, or call-out boxes to call attention to the most important messages on each slide

Practice

1. Pick a product from a company that you are interviewing with. Prepare a presentation proposing how you would improve the product. Your presentation can have a maximum of 10 slides, including the title slide.

2. Pick a company that you are interviewing with. Analyze a competitor's product, including its strengths, weaknesses, and opportunities for improvement. Your presentation can have a maximum of 8 slides, including the title slide.

3. Pick a company that you are interviewing with. Prepare a presentation on a new product that you believe the company should launch. Explain why the company should create it and provide an overview of the key product features. Your presentation can have a maximum of 15 slides, including the title slide.

Solutions

1. Pick a product from a company that you are interviewing with. Prepare a presentation proposing how you would improve the product. Your presentation can have a maximum of 10 slides, including the title slide.

   Here is one potential structure you could use to make your presentation slides:

   - *Title*
   - *Executive summary*
   - *Identify a customer segment to focus on*
   - *Identify pain points to focus on*
   - *Evaluate different product improvement ideas*
   - *Recommendation for improvement #1*
   - *Recommendation for improvement #2*
   - *Recommendation for improvement #3*
   - *Risks & mitigations*
   - *Next steps*

2. Pick a company that you are interviewing with. Analyze a competitor's product, including its strengths, weaknesses, and opportunities for improvement. Your presentation can have a maximum of 8 slides, including the title slide.

   Here is one potential structure you could use to make your presentation slides:

   - *Title*

- *Executive summary*
- *Identify a product to focus on*
- *Product strengths*
- *Product weaknesses*
- *Evaluate different product improvement ideas*
- *Recommendation for product improvements*
- *Risks & mitigations / next steps*

3. Pick a company that you are interviewing with. Prepare a presentation on a new product that you believe the company should launch. Explain why the company should create it and provide an overview of the key product features. Your presentation can have a maximum of 15 slides, including the title slide.

   Here is one potential structure you could use to make your presentation slides:

   - *Title*
   - *Executive summary*
   - *Market analysis (e.g., market size, growth rate)*
   - *Major competitor products and alternatives*
   - *Unmet customer pain points and opportunities*
   - *Overview of the new product*
   - *Product key feature #1*
   - *Product key feature #2*

- *Product key feature #3*
- *Potential synergies with the company's existing products*
- *Other product ideas that were considered*
- *Product development roadmap*
- *Product marketing plan*
- *Risks & mitigations*
- *Next steps*

Bonus Tip: If you have the time, get a PM friend or colleague to take a look at your take-home assignment. They will likely have valuable constructive feedback to give you.

14. Conclusion

Summary

In this chapter, we'll go through a summary of everything we've covered. There is a lot of material presented in this book, so it may be helpful to revisit certain sections that you may have forgotten.

We covered the following topics:

- Conducting company research
- Define yourself questions
- Motivational questions
- Behavioral questions
- Product questions
- Marketing questions
- Estimation questions

- Strategy questions
- Metrics questions
- Execution questions
- Technical questions
- Take-home assignments

Conducting company research

- Essential information you should know about the company includes:
    - What is the company's mission statement or aspiration?
    - What are the company's products and services?
    - What is the company's business model?
    - Who are the company's customers?
    - Who are the company's competitors?
- Use a SWOT analysis to build a perspective on the company
    - **Strengths**: What does the company do well? What qualities differentiate them from competitors?
    - **Weaknesses**: What does the company do poorly? What are the things that competitors do better?
    - **Opportunities**: Where are the opportunities for growth or improvement?
    - **Threats**: Who are the most threatening competitors? What are the major risks to the company's business?

- You should also research the specific role and team you are interviewing for:
  - What are the responsibilities or tasks of the role?
  - What skills or attributes are preferred or required?
  - How does the role fit with the broader organization?
  - What are the primary goals or targets of the team?
  - What is the culture of the team and company like?

Define yourself questions

- Define yourself questions ask about your professional identity, including your skills, qualities, values, and goals
- How to answer "Walk me through your resume"
  - Start with a strong opening statement that summarizes your areas of expertise and number of years of experience
  - Highlight your most relevant and impressive experiences and accomplishments, starting with the most recent
  - Connect your experiences to why you're interested in the role and why you would be a good fit
- How to answer "What is your greatest strength?"
  - Provide a one sentence, high-level summary of your greatest strength
  - Illustrate your strength with an example
  - Explain how this strength will help you as a product manager

- How to answer "What is your greatest weakness?"
    - Provide a one sentence, high-level summary of your greatest weakness
    - Illustrate your weakness with an example
    - Explain the specific steps you have taken to improve on this weakness
    - Describe the tangible outcomes as a result of your improvement
    - Reflect on your progress and what you have learned and what you have left to learn or practice
- How to answer "Where do you see yourself in 5-10 years?"
    - Provide a one sentence, high-level summary of the role or position you aspire towards
    - Describe the impact you would make in this role or position
    - Explain how the skills and insights you would gain in the current role you are interviewing for will help you in your career trajectory
- How to answer "Why should we hire you?"
    - "You should hire me for the following three reasons"
    - "One…" [Example]
    - "Two…" [Example]
    - "Three…" [Example]

  - "For these reasons, I believe that I would be a great fit for the role and would be able to make an immediate, tangible impact on the company"

- How to answer "Why are you leaving your current job?"
  - Answer in a positive tone; avoid speaking negatively about your current or previous employer
  - Emphasize professional growth as the main reason for leaving your current job

- How to answer "What do you do in your free time?"
  - Give an authentic answer; do not make up specific hobbies or interests because you think that is what the interviewers want to hear
  - Strike a balance between personal and professional interests
  - Emphasize continuous learning and growth

Motivational questions

- How to answer "Why are you interested in product management?"
  - Use the structure: "I am interested in product management for three reasons. One… Two… Three… Given these interests, I believe product management is the perfect fit for me"
  - Your reasons should focus on the responsibilities and the potential impact of being a PM

- How to answer "Why do you want to work at this company?"

- Use the structure: "[Company Name] is a top choice for me for three reasons. One… Two… Three… For these reasons, I would love to work for [Company Name]"
- If the company is truly your number one choice, make sure to state it in your first sentence
- If the company has a strong mission or core value, ensure you mention it in your answer

Behavioral questions

- Prepare 6 – 8 different stories drawn upon your past professional and personal experiences
- Ensure that your stories are collectively diverse and cover a variety of different themes, such as: leadership, teamwork, problem solving, resilience, integrity, decision making, communication, and interpersonal skills
- When asked a behavioral question, mentally run through your prepared list of stories and select the one that is the most relevant that you have not shared yet
- Structure your answer using the SPAR method
    - **Summary**: Provide a one-sentence summary of the story that you are about to tell the interviewer
    - **Problem**: Describe the problem you encountered or were asked to solve
    - **Action**: Explain what steps you took to handle the task or to meet the goal or objective
    - **Result**: Describe the outcome that your actions had, quantifying the impact and effect you had on the organization

Product questions

- There are three common product questions:
    - What is your favorite product and why?
    - What is your least favorite product and why?
    - How would you design or improve a particular product?
- When picking a favorite product, make sure that it adheres to these five principles:
    - The product is one that you know well
    - The product is complex enough
    - The product is not ubiquitous
    - The product is not too obscure or niche
    - The product is relevant to the company
- You can use the following structure to answer the "what's your favorite product?" and "what's your least favorite product?" questions
    - "[Product] is my [favorite/least favorite] product"
    - "[1-2 sentence summary of what the product does]"
    - "There are three reasons why this product is my [favorite/least favorite]: [reason 1], [reason 2], [reason 3]"
    - "[Reason 1]…"
    - "[Reason 2]…"

  - "[Reason 3]…"
  - "For these reasons, I believe this is a [great/poor] product"
- There are six main steps in answering product improvement and design questions
  - Define the goal
  - Identify a customer segment to target
  - Select a pain point to focus on
  - Brainstorm product improvements or designs
  - Assess which idea is best
  - Explain how you would test this
- The SCAMPER framework can help you brainstorm new product ideas
  - Substitute
  - Combine
  - Adapt
  - Modify
  - Put to another use
  - Eliminate
  - Reverse

Marketing questions

- The STP framework helps identify a customer segment and positioning statement for your product
  - **Segmentation**: Create a list of customer segments
  - **Targeting**: Select one segment to focus on
  - **Positioning**: Decide how to position and communicate the product
- The 4 P's framework helps define the best way to market a product
  - **Product**: Decide which product or version of the product to market
  - **Place**: Decide where the product will be sold
  - **Promotion**: Decide how to spread information about the product to customers
  - **Price**: Decide how to price the product

Estimation questions

- Estimation questions ask you to estimate a particular number or figure by making assumptions and performing calculations
- One of the most common types of estimation questions are market sizing questions, which ask you to estimate the annual spending of a specific category of product
- For estimation questions, you are evaluated on whether you can take a logical, structured approach and whether you are comfortable dealing with numbers
- There are two methods to tackle estimation questions

  - In a top-down approach, start with a large number and then refine and break down the number until you get your answer
  - In a bottom-up approach, start with a small number and then build up and increase the number until you get your answer

- There are three strategies to make reasonable assumptions:
  - Use personal experiences
  - Use a proxy
  - Use lower and upper bounds

- Follow these estimation math tips to simplify your math calculations and greatly decrease the chances that you make a mistake:
  - Work with units instead of numbers
  - Use the distributive property
  - Round numbers
  - Use factors of numbers
  - Reverse percentages
  - Sense check numbers along the way

Strategy questions

- A framework is a tool to structure and break down business problems into smaller components
- There are six steps to creating outstanding frameworks to answer strategy questions

- Memorize eight robust business categories: market, competition, company, product, customer, profitability, alternatives, and risks
- When asked a business strategy question, ask for a few minutes to structure your thoughts
- Mentally run through the eight business categories and select the 3-4 most relevant ones
- If you are unable to select 3-4 relevant business categories, think of your own business categories to include
- Add specific questions under each business category you've selected
- Walk the interviewer through your framework and answer

Metrics questions

- Metrics questions ask you to determine what metrics you would look at when analyzing the performance of a product, feature, or business decision
- A key performance indicator, or KPI for short, is a measurable value that evaluates the performance of a company, product, or individual over time
- Some of the most common KPIs for product managers include:
    - Customer acquisition cost (CAC)
    - Conversion rate
    - Customer lifetime value (CLV)
    - Average revenue per user (ARPU)

  - Churn rate
  - Retention rate
  - Yearly/monthly/daily active users (YAU, MAU, DAU)
  - Net Promoter Score (NPS)
- There are three steps to answering metrics questions
  - Identify which qualities are most important
  - Brainstorm potential metrics for each quality
  - Select metrics that are accurate and feasibly measured

Execution questions

- There are three common types of execution questions:
  - Investigating a metric
  - A/B testing questions
  - Optimizing a flow or funnel
- To answer questions on investigating a metric:
  - Compare against the right historical data
  - Check against competitors or the industry
  - Look at the metric by different segments
  - Identify the root cause of the issue
  - Brainstorm potential solutions
  - Propose a plan to test or implement your solution

- To answer A/B testing questions:
    - Define your objective and hypothesis
    - Identify your variable and versions
    - Determine sample size
    - Randomly assign participants
    - Set up data tracking
    - Analyze the results of the A/B test
- To answer questions on optimizing a flow or funnel:
    - Identify all of the steps in a customer flow
    - Identify which steps are underperforming
    - Brainstorm potential solutions
    - Propose a plan to test or implement your solution

Technical questions

- Technical questions assess your understanding of technical concepts relevant to the product you'd be managing
- Common technical concepts that are fundamental to being a PM that you should be familiar with include:
    - Basic programming concepts
    - Basic algorithms
    - Web technologies
    - Database fundamentals

- APIs
- System architecture and design
- Agile / scrum methodologies

Take-home assignments

- How to complete take-home assignments
  - Read the instructions carefully
  - Ask clarifying questions
  - Research and gather information
  - Create an outline
  - Create your slides
  - Proofread and review
  - Prepare for the presentation
- You can use the following structure when making your presentation slides
  - Title
  - Executive summary
  - Supporting analysis slides
  - Recommendation / summary
  - Risks & mitigations
  - Next steps
  - Appendix

- Follow these best practices when creating slides to make your presentation clear and easy to understand
    - Write descriptive slide titles that communicate the main message of the slide
    - All of the titles of your slides should collectively read like a story
    - Avoid overcrowding your slides by having only one key message for each slide
    - Use a variety of slide formats, such as bullets, charts, graphs, tables, diagrams, and mockups
    - Use bolding, circles, boxes, color, or call-out boxes to call attention to the most important messages on each slide

Final Thoughts

Congratulations on making it through this book!

You now know exactly what to expect for product manager interviews. You know the types of questions your interviewers will ask, what they are looking for, and step-by-step strategies on how to answer each question.

You have all of the information you need to succeed. The strategies in this book have already helped give you a competitive edge over the average applicant.

The next step is to practice using all of the strategies you have learned in this book. Practice is what separates candidates that land multiple PM job offers from candidates that don't receive any.

For questions that you know you will get asked, take the time to carefully prepare answers to them. These are easy opportunities for you to make a great impression on your interviewer.

For the other types of questions, do enough practice questions until you feel confident and relaxed when answering them.

Preparing for PM interviews takes a lot of time and effort, but the investment is worth it to land a fulfilling and high-paying job.

I wish you the best of luck!

15. About the Author

Taylor Warfield

Taylor Warfield is a former Bain Manager and interviewer. He is the founder of HackingTheCaseInterview.com and author of "Hacking The Case Interview" and "The Ultimate Case Interview Workbook."

His books, online course, and coaching have helped thousands of students and working professionals land job offers in consulting, business, and tech.

Made in the USA
Las Vegas, NV
14 February 2024

85805800R00154